Modern Indian Literature

Modern Indian Literature

Edited by and for
the Department of English
University of Delhi

OXFORD
UNIVERSITY PRESS

Oxford University Press is a department of the University of Oxford. It furthers the University's objective of excellence in research, scholarship, and education by publishing worldwide. Oxford is a registered trade mark of Oxford University Press in the UK and in certain other countries

Published in India by
Oxford University Press
22 Workspace, 2nd Floor, 1/22 Asaf Ali Road, New Delhi 110 002

First published 1999
27th impression 2022

ISBN-13: 978-0-19-565118-8
ISBN-10: 0-19-565118-9

Printed in India by Rakmo Press, New Delhi 110 020

For product information and current price, please visit www.india.oup.com

PREFACE

As English has become more and more a global language, it has more and more become a vehicle for World Literature. Numerous writers from diverse and disparate regions from all over the world have adopted it as their preferred medium of creative expression, and other (surely still more numerous) writers who continue to create in a language other than English are becoming widely available in English translation.

The neo-colonization effected through a global use of English has thus served, in a happy paradox, also to bring about a decolonization of literary studies in a country like ours. English Literature, i.e. literature written in English by English/British authors, the systematic study of which was introduced and promoted in India for well over a hundred years under colonial aegis (and which as our 'master' literature catalyzed the growth of modern literature in nearly all the major Indian languages), is now seen to be just one national literature among many, no more distinguished or valuable necessarily than the literatures of many other countries of the world which have had a comparably long and rich literary tradition.

In order to recognize, reflect and indeed disseminate these developments, the new syllabus for the BA (Honours) course in English of the University of Delhi now includes (besides several papers in literature and literary theory from various parts of the world), an entire compulsory paper in Indian Literature to be studied in the Ist Year. This anthology brings together six short stories and selections from the five poets prescribed in Units 4 and 5 of this paper. These include the works of both Indian writers writing originally in English and those writing in a variety of Indian languages—Bengali, Hindi, Malayalam, Tamil, Telugu and Urdu—but to be read here in English translation. (This paper includes, besides this anthology, a novel from Bengali in English translation, *Home and the World (Ghare Baire)* by Rabindranath Tagore; another novel written originally in English, *The Shadow Lines* by Amitav Ghosh; and two plays in English translation from Hindi and Marathi respectively, *Halfway House (Adhe Adhure)* by Mohan Rakesh, and *Ghashiram Kotwal* by Vijay Tendulkar.

It gives me great pleasure to thank all our 600-odd colleagues in the various colleges of the University of Delhi who facilitated the adoption of the new syllabus and some of whom then came forward to assist in the editing of this anthology. The work of each of the eleven writers in this anthology was edited by a colleague with expertise in the area, including familiarity with the original literary tradition in the case of translated texts, and their contributions were co-ordinated by a committee comprising some members of the Department of English, University of Delhi. All these colleagues are named on the next page and to them in particular I extend my warmest gratitude.

HARISH TRIVEDI
Head
Department of English

University of Delhi

EDITORS

Dilip Kumar Basu — *Jibanananda Das*
Rajdhani College

Anupama Prabhala Kapse — *Sri Sri*
Gargi College

Shyam Sundar Sharma — *G. M. Muktibodh*
Motilal Nehru College (Evening)

Madhu Grover — *Nissim Ezekiel*
Lady Shri Ram College

Mahasweta Baxipatra — *Jayanta Mahapatra*
Gargi College

Anand Prakash — *Premchand*
Hans Raj College

Ranga Rao — *R. K. Narayan*
Sri Venkateswara College

Vanajam Ravindran — *Vaikom Muhammad Basheer*
Lady Shri Ram College (retired)

Sukrita Paul Kumar — *Saadat Hasan Manto*
Zakir Husain College

Rashmi Govind — *Ismat Chughtai*
Zakir Husain College

B. Mangalam — *Ambai*
Ram Lal Anand College (Evening)

Coordinated by
Manju Jain
(Convener)

Shormishtha Panja Udaya Kumar

ACKNOWLEDGEMENTS

The editors and publishers of this anthology are grateful to the following for permission to reprint material which they published originally, or for which they hold copyright. Copyright holders who could not be contacted earlier because of lack of information are requested to correspond with Oxford University Press, New Delhi.

Sahitya Akademi and Sukanta Chaudhuri for 'Before Dying', 'Windy Night', 'I Shall Return to this Bengal' by Jibanananda Das.

Indian Council for Cultural Relations for 'Forward March' by Sri Sri.

V. Narayana Rao for 'Some People Laugh, Some People Cry' by Sri Sri.

Penguin Books for 'So Very Far' by G. M. Muktibodh.

Jayanta Mahapatra for 'Hunger', 'Dhauli', 'A Country' and 'Grandfather'.

Vikas Publishing House for 'The Holy Panchayat' by Premchand.

R. K. Narayan for 'The "M. C. C."'

'The Card-Sharper's Daughter' was first published in Malayalam as 'Mucheettukalikkarante Makal' in 1951. This translation by K. M. Sherrif appeared in 1996 in *Short Stories: Vaikom Muhammad Basheer* published by Katha.

Indian Institute of Advanced Study for 'Toba Tek Singh'.

Ashish Sawhny for 'Lihaf (The Quilt) by Ismat Chughtai.

East West Books for 'The Squirrel' by Ambai.

CONTENTS

I. Poems

JIBANANANDA DAS

(1899–1954)

Jibanananda Das is regarded today by many as the most important poet in Bengali after Tagore, and a participant in what is widely considered a 'Modernist' movement in Bengali poetry which began in the 1930s. Buddhadeva Bose, Bishnu Dey, Amiya Chakravarty, Sudhindranath Datta and Premendra Mitra are some of the other names mentioned in this connection. Although they had widely different approaches, most critics have found an orchestrated voice in the poetry created by this group, at least in the initial period. Critical opinion notices a decisive movement away from the existing language of Bengali poetry, a shift from the prevalent literary culture, and an expression of a 'tortured sensibility' in this 'adhunik kabita' or 'modernist poetry'.

Jibanananda was born in Barishal (now in Bangladesh), and grew up in a lush green environment which houses its unique set of birds, beasts and insects. Ponds and rivers were many, and even the sea was close by. The poet, always something of a loner, apparently watched these natural phenomena with fascination. His school teacher father, Satyananda, was active in social and religious organizations and his mother, Kusumkumari, was a poet. Jibanananda was introduced to English Literature quite early in his life. He studied English at Presidency College, Calcutta, and at the University of Calcutta, and taught English Literature in various colleges, including Ramjas College, Delhi. In between, there were periods of unemployment and financial distress. In 1946, the year of the 'Calcutta riots', while teaching in Brajamohan College, Barishal, Jibanananda was in Calcutta on a holiday and had to postpone returning to Barishal. When the country was partitioned the following year Jibanananda stayed back in Calcutta. He continued to live and write there, although he remained nostalgic for that part of Bengal to which he could not return. Aloof and meditative, he avoided noisy crowds and literary gatherings. His outstanding poetic abilities were recognized only by a handful of people during his lifetime, and a great deal of his poetry was anthologized and published posthumously. Jibanananda died on 22 October 1954, eight days after he was hit by a tram-car in Calcutta. His novels and short stories, published long after his death, startled readers. It was not only the unusual nature and quality of these works that was surprising: few expected the sheer volume of his prose fiction which includes *Jalpaihati, Malyaban, Sutirtha* and *Basmatir Upakhyan* (all written in 1948).

The poet had started publishing in the twenties. By the early thirties he had transformed the traditional Bengali metre, 'payar', into a hesitant, gentle rhythm with pauses. (The 'payar' is the most extensively used metre in Bengali poetry in which each line consists of 14 morae or units of metrical time equal to the duration of a short syllable, with a caesura after the eighth mora). Jibanananda made 'payar' an effective vehicle for the expression of a consciousness worrying about and weary of both personal and general human destiny, but sometimes also registering bewildered ecstasy. The tag of 'the loneliest poet' attached to Jibanananda by some early admirers of this phase of his work has stuck, and not without justification. The three poems included here were written during this phase. In his early years Jibanananda felt alienated from the rest of humanity. Later, this estrangement was no longer his subject: there remained only the lonely melancholy of one who has meditated deeper and longer than his fellow-men on the human condition. A sense of history pervades much of his work and occupies the central place in his later poems, as in the collection *Bela, Abela, Kalbela* (Time, Wrong Time, Inauspicious Time, 1961), where he even changes his old practised metre to one with more buoyancy in order to accommodate hope. Jibanananda once wrote that while people had variously assessed his poetry as 'the poetry of loneliness', 'nature-poetry', 'the poetry of historical and social consciousness', or 'poetry in the symbolic tradition', he himself was of the view that all these descriptions were correct, but only partially. A particular poem or a phrase of his might invite one or other of these labels, but none would suit the entire corpus.

Jibanananda has a fascination for grass, for certain bushes and shrubs, for owls, vultures and ducks, for the jackal, the rat, the firefly and the cricket. He paints his landscapes in ways that make the everyday world look unfamiliar, replete as it is with messages and signals of other times. He sees extraordinary shades of colour, both soft and dazzling, and is obsessed with all kinds of smell. In his poems on Bengal, Jibanananda constantly remembers Bengali home-made sweets, embroidery, traditional lore, and the sounds of 'kirtan' and of rivers flowing as banks collapse on either side. He sometimes speaks of flights across a vast space just beyond the margins of the usual layers of reality, as in 'Windy Night'. A consciousness of death—of individuals and of civilizations—recurs in his poetry, as is evident in all the three poems included in this anthology.

Some of Jibanananda's major poetry has been included in *Dhusar Pandulipi* (The Grey Manuscript, 1936); *Mahaprithivi* (The Great Earth, 1944); *Sat-ti Tarar Timir* (The Darkness of Seven Stars, 1948); *Banalata Sen* (1942); *Rupasi Bangla* (Beautiful Bengal, 1957); and *Bela, Abela, Kalbela* (Time, Wrong Time, Inauspicious Time, 1961). 'Before Dying' ('Mrityur Age'), first published in 1935, is included in *Dhusar Pandulipi* (1930). 'Windy Night' ('Haoar Rat'), first published in 1936, is included in *Banalata Sen* (1942). 'I shall return to this Bengal' ('Abar Asiba Phire'), written in 1934 and published posthumously in *Rupasi Bangla* (1957), is one of the many sonnets that Jibanananda wrote on Bengal. The rhyme–scheme of this Bengali sonnet is abbaabbacdcdee. All the poems included here are thus from Jibanananda's early period, the 1930s and the 1940s. The translations reproduced below are from *A Certain Sense* (New Delhi: Sahitya Akademi, 1998). Other translated versions of these poems may be found in *Jibanananda Das,* translated by Chidananda Das Gupta (New Delhi: Sahitya Akademi, 1972).

BEFORE DYING

We who have walked in winter dusk through lonely stubble-fields,
Have seen at field's-end soft river-women strewing flowers
Of mist; like village girls are they, alas, of long ago;
We who have seen in darkness the akanda, dhundhul trees
Fill with glowworms; and, at the head of a fallow field,
The moon stand silent, uncaring of harvest-yield;

We who have loved the long winter night in darkness,
Have heard on roof-thatch wings beating in the tranced night;
The old owl-smell—lost again, ah where, in the darkness!
Wonderful the winter night, we know—full of the deep delight
Of wings gliding over fields; herons calling from peepul-boughs;
We who have learned these hidden enchantments of life;

We who have seen the wild duck, escaping the hunter's shot
Take wing into the horizon's mild blue moonlit glow,
We who have rested our hands in love on the paddy-sheaf,
And come home like evening crows, expectantly; have found
Children's breath-scent, grass, sun, kingfishers, stars, sky—
Traces of these, again and again, the whole year round;

We have seen the green leaf yellowing in the autumn dark;
Light and bulbuls play in windows of hijal-branches;
The mouse on winter nights coat its silk fur with bits of grain;
Morning and evening, to the eyes of lonely fish, the ripples
Fall fair in smoky rice-smell; at pond's edge the duck at dusk
Smells sleep and is borne away by a soft female hand.

Clouds like minarets call golden kites to their windows;
Under the cane creepers, the sparrows' eggs are hard;
The river coats the bank with the soft water's smell;
In dense night the roof-thatch shadow falls on the moonlit yard,
Smell of crickets in the air—green air of summer fields,
In deep desire thick juice descends to the blue annona's core.

We who have seen, under the dense banyan, the red fruit lie
Fallen; lonely fields crowd to see their faces in the river,
The blue skies that remain seek the depths of other blue skies,
Along the paths soft eyes cast shadows on the earth,
We who have seen evening alight from rows of areca-palms
Daily; each day the dawn like paddy-sheaves come green and calm;

We who have learnt: after days, months, seasons had passed,
That daughter of earth drew near to tell us the rivers' tales

In darkness; we who have sensed within banks and fields and paths
There is another light, on its body the afternoon dust:
Loosing its hold on eyesight, that light is calm and still; there
Earth's Kankavati drifts into a body of faded incense.

What more would we know before death? Do we not know, alas,
At the head of all roseate desire like a blank wall there wakes
Death's grey face: all the dreams, the gold the world once had
Pass into unresponsive peace—as though a sorceress makes
Use of them; what more would we know? Have we not heard birds cry;
After the sunlight fades; in meadow mists, seen the crows fly?

Translated from the Bengali
by Supriya Chaudhuri

WINDY NIGHT

Last night was a night of deep winds—a night of countless stars.

Throughout the night
The expansive wind played round my mosquito-net—
The net swelled at times like the monsoon ocean's belly;
Sometimes the bedclothes were torn apart
And wished to fly towards the stars.
At times it seemed to me—perhaps in a half-sleep—
The net was not above me;
It was flying like a white heron on the ocean of blue winds,
Brushing Swati's lap.
Last night was such an amazing night!

All the dead stars woke up—there was no empty space in the sky.
Among those stars I saw the ashen face
Of all the earth's dead loved ones.
The stars gleamed, as in the dark night
The dewy eyes of the male lover-kite atop the peepul tree.

The vast sky glowed in the moonlight like the bright leopardskin stole
Across the shoulders of a Babylonian Queen.
Last night was such an amazing night!

The stars who had died in the sky's lap thousands of years ago,
They too came through the window, bringing with them countless dead skies.
The beauties I had seen dying in Assyria, Egypt, Vidisa,
Seemed to stand ranked on the faraway frontiers of the skies,
Among the mists, with long spears in their hands.
Was it to trample down death?
Was it to express the deep-felt triumph of life?
Was it to raise a stern fearsome tower of love?

I am benumbed—overwhelmed,
As if torn apart by last night's fierce blue torture;
Amid the limitless outspread wings of the sky,
The earth was razed out last night like a grub.
And the lofty wind from the bosom of the sky
Came whistling through the window
Like countless zebras on the green plain, scattered by the lion's roar.

My heart is filled with the scent of green grass on the sprawling veldt,
With the scent of robust horizon-flooding sunlight,
With the vast, restless, animate, shaggy outpourings of the dark
Like the roar of a sex-charged tigress,
With the undaunted blue madness of life.

My heart flew away, tearing the earth asunder,
Like a blown-up drunken balloon in the sea of blue wind—
Carrying with it, like an indomitable vulture,
From star to star, the mast of a distant star.

Translated from the Bengali
by Ujjwal Kumar Majumdar

I SHALL RETURN TO THIS BENGAL

I shall return to this Bengal, to the Dhansiri's bank:
Perhaps not as a man, but myna or fishing-kite;
Or dawn crow, floating on the mist's bosom to alight
In the shade of this jackfruit tree, in this autumn harvest-land.
Or maybe a duck—a young girl's—bells on my red feet,
Drifting on kalmi-scented waters all the day:
For love of Bengal's rivers, fields, crops, I'll come this way
To this sad green shore of Bengal, drenched by the Jalangi's waves.

Perhaps you'll see a glass-fly ride the evening breeze,
Or hear a barn owl call from the silk-cotton tree;
A little child toss rice-grains on the courtyard grass,
Or a boy on the Rupsa's turgid stream steer a dinghy
With torn white sail—white egrets swimming through red clouds
To their home in the dark. You will find me among their crowd.

Translated from the Bengali
by Sukanta Chaudhuri

ANNOTATIONS

'Before Dying'

Lines 2–3
soft river-women: They are virtually like river-sprites.
flowers/Of mist: The small masses of fog coming out of the river assume an iridescence in this phrase, somewhat muted by the 'alas' in the following line. The poem subtly and continuously plays beauty, desire, life and colour against grey death.

Line 21
bits of grain: Bits of rice; Bengali 'khud'.

Line 23
smoky rice-smell: Caused by rice being washed in the pond for the day's use in various homes.

Line 29
summer: 'Baisakh', the first month of the Bengali summer, in the original.

Line 30
annona: The notes in *A Certain Sense* explain that it is a fruit related to the custard apple. The Bengali word is 'nona'.

Line 33
The blue skies that remain... : The feeling evoked in the original is that these skies feel forsaken.

Line 42
Earth's Kankavati: 'In folk legend, a young girl whose brother vows to marry any woman who would eat a certain mango. A tragic situation arises when Kankavati unwittingly eats the fruit. Finally, she drifts on a boat to an unknown realm: the implication is that she dies' *(A Certain Sense).*

Lines 47–8
Use of them... crows fly?: The original Bengali poem has in each stanza the rhyme-scheme *ababcc.* The couplet at the end of the poem in the original has sharp rhyming words, and produces the effect of a sudden severance, a snapping of some tie. With the visual image of the sudden flight of the crows in the gathering mist, the poem closes on the note of death.

'Windy Night'

Line 3
mosquito-net: The mosquito-net is personified in the original poem. It wishes to tear itself away from the bed.

Line 9
a white heron: 'A white crane'; 'shada bok' in Bengali. The word 'bok' can also mean egret.

Line 10
Swati: 'The star Arcturus, held to be an auspicious star, especially for meetings and unions. It is said that a raindrop landing on an oyster turns to a pearl when Swati is in the sky' (*A Certain Sense).*

Line 16
the male lover-kite: The word 'chilpurush' in the original poem is an unusual one coined by the poet. It gives the kite a legendary/mythical touch.

Line 18
a Babylonian Queen: Babylon was one of the most famous cities of the ancient world. It was the capital of southern Mesopotamia (Babylonia), which is now a part of Iraq, from the early second millennium to the early first millennium BC. It later became an independent city-state and rose to its greatest glory in the sixth century BC. The histories of the Babylonian and Assyrian kingdoms are closely connected as they controlled the fertile region between the rivers Tigris and Euphrates at one time or another.

Line 22
Assyria: The kingdom of northern Mesopotamia that became the centre of one of the great empires of the Middle East. In the seventh century BC even Egypt became a part of it. It was located in what is now northern Iraq and southeastern Turkey. The power struggle between Babylon and Assyria began around 2000 BC and continued for nearly 1500 years. Assyria was a dependency of Babylonia during most of the second millennium BC. It emerged as an independent state in the fourteenth century BC. The Assyrians were famous for their fighting prowess. They also built the famous archaeological sites at Nineveh and Nimrud.

Egypt: The Egyptian civilization in the Nile valley dates back to the Old Stone Age. The land of Egypt was united around 3100 BC. It ultimately declined after becoming a part of the Roman Empire in 30 BC.

Vidisa: A famous city in ancient India that arose between 200 BC and 300 AD. It was the capital of the Dasharanya kingdom in the south-east of the Vindhyas. The ivory workers' guild at Vidisa carved the stone sculpture on the gateways and railings around the Sanchi stupa.

The references to Assyria, Egypt and Vidisha, as also the earlier reference to Babylon, are typical of Jibanananda. His consciousness of history and of the flow of time often find expression in lines which mention ancient civilizations.

Lines 23–4
Seemed to stand... in their hands: The Bengali original has one very long line, not two, which has its own special effect.

Line 31
grub: The Bengali word in the original translates literally as 'worm' or 'small insect'.

'I shall return to this Bengal'

Line 1
Dhansiri: A river in Jibanananda's native Barishal.

Line 2
fishing kite: This bird is also called the Brahminy kite.

Line 4
this autumn harvest-land: This is late autumn, 'Kartik' (roughly 16 October to 15 November), the month specified in the Bengali original.

Line 6
kalmi-scented: This reed is abundantly found along the edges of the ponds in Bengal. It is also eaten in Bengal, especially in villages, and thus has a place in domesticity.

Line 8
Jalangi: A river running through the Murshidabad and Nadia districts of Bengal.

Line 9
glass-fly: The Bengali word here is 'sudarshan'. 'Glass-fly' is the usual translation for the Bengali 'kanch-poka'. A 'sudarshan' with red and white dots on its wings is different from a 'kanch-poka', a common species of green beetle in Bengal. See Bibhutibhushan Bandyopadhyay, *Pather Panchali,* chapter 18:
Bu-u-u-u- there was a sound. A glass-fly!

—No, not a glass-fly, but a 'sudarshan'... tiny white and red dots on its wings as if sandal-paste got sprinkled on them.

Sudarshan—It is not an insect actually—a god. She [Durga] has heard from her mother, as well as from many others, that it is a special blessing to have seen one. Sudarshan, please keep us in happiness and comfort (exactly the words she has heard others utter)... On the dust the insect... was going round and round...

(Editor's translation)

Line 12

Rupsa: A river in what is now Bangladesh.
turgid: This is probably a printing error. The word should be turbid, meaning muddy.

SUGGESTED REA DING

Bose, Buddhadeva, *An Acre of Green Grass* (1948), Calcutta: Papyrus, 1982.

Chaudhuri, Sukanta ed., *A Certain Sense: Poems by Jibanananda Das,* New Delhi: Sahitya Akademi, 1998.

Das Gupta, Chidananda, *Jibanananda Das,* New Delhi: Sahitya Akademi, 1972.

Seely, Clinton B., *A Poet Apart: A Literary Biography of the Bengali Poet Jibanananda Das (1899–1954),* Newark: University of Delaware Press, 1990, rpt. Calcutta: Rabindra Bharati University, 1999.

Sen, Anjan and Seethalakshmi Vishwanath eds, *'gaNgeo pOttro', Collection,* 16 (Jibanananda Das Birth Centenary Memorial Issue), 1999.

SRI SRI

(1910–83)

Srirangam Srinivasa Rao (Sri Sri) was born in Visakhapatnam, in what is now Andhra Pradesh. By the time he finished school, he had already composed poems in traditional verse forms and written a detective novel, *Parinaya Rahasyamu* (Wedding Secret, 1925). His first collection of poems, *Prabhava* (Birth/Awakening, 1928), was influenced by the English romantic poets. As an undergraduate in Madras, he read Edgar Allan Poe, Guy de Maupassant and A. C. Swinburne, and even translated some poems of Charles Baudelaire. 'Jayabheri' (Victory Song, 1933) marks a clear break from his experiments with 'bhava kavitvamu' (romantic poetry) which by then was a spent force in Telugu poetry. A fresh idiom was required to articulate a different poetic agenda, namely to recover and define the experience of the masses which was not subjective but collective. By this time Sri Sri had come under the influence of the English progressive poetry of Cecil Day Lewis and W. H. Auden. He had also translated the work of Indian revolutionary poets such as Kazi Nazrul Islam and Harindranath Chattopadhyaya.

Kazi Nazrul Islam's 'Chal, Chal, Chal' (Marching Song) directly influenced the writing of 'Mahaprasthanam' (The Great Departure, 1934). Its inspiration also came from the success of the Russian Revolution and Sri Sri's exposure to Communist literature and ideology. The new poetry came to be known as 'abhyudaya kavitvamu' (progressive poetry) and it was Sri Sri who was its most powerful exponent. The working class movement also gained momentum through the covert circulation of its literature in the Andhra and Madras districts in the years 1929–30. Journals such as *Jwala* (Flame), founded by S. Muddukrishna, where 'Mahaprasthanam' was first published, provided a forum for disseminating the message of a free, classless society devoid of conflict, thus inspiring people to fight oppression. The Communist Party of India and the Congress Socialist Party were formed in 1934. The first Conference of the Abhyudaya Rachayitula Sangham (Arasam) or the Progressive Poets' Association was held in Tenali in 1943, and Sri Sri was to be its President for many years. In the 1940s, Sri Sri came to be known not only as a formidable poet but also as a political activist. New creative experiments with surrealism are evident in his poetry of this period. He translated Andre Breton's *Surrealist Manifesto* in 1945, and also the poems of Paul Eluard, Apollinaire and Salvador Dali. The poems of this period were later published in the collection entitled *Khadga Srushti* (The Creation of the Sword, 1966). This collection was preceded by *Maroprapancham* (Another World, 1954), *Charama Ratri* (Final Night, 1957) and *Moodu Yabhaylu* (Three Fifties, 1964), and followed by *Maroprasthanam* (Another Departure, 1977). The large body of work left by Sri Sri also includes criticism, essays and letters. Sri Sri became President of the Viplava Rachayitula Sangham (Virasam) or the Revolutionary Poets' Association in 1970 and he received the Sahitya Akademi Award in 1972.

'Mahaprasthanam' lent its title to Sri Sri's second collection of poems (1950). The English version, 'Forward March', translated by the poet, appeared in the collection *Three Cheers for Man* (1956). This was later published in the *Sri Sri Miscellany* (1970). It combined influences as diverse as Adi Shankara and Wilfred Owen, ushering in a new epoch in Telugu literature and influencing an entire generation of poets. Its quick, racy metre displays technical dexterity of enormous power. Like most of the poems in the collection, 'Mahaprasthanam' is meant to be sung rather than read. Its economy of expression, its usage of simple, everyday speech patterns, and its keen sense of lived life became hallmarks of progressive poetry. 'A pup/ a match/ or a cake of soap/ are not to be looked down upon/ for they are all poetry', he wrote in the poem 'Rikkulu' (Unquenchable). According to Sri Sri, the social function of art came first and foremost. The themes of journey and revolution are intertwined not only in 'Forward March' but also in the entire range of songs. His readers are 'comrades' who must join the great march. The synthesis of modernism, myth and tradition imparts a compelling intensity to the poem and hints at an original sensibility at work. Continual experiments with form, in addition to Sri Sri's travels and the experience of World War II, informed the writing of the collection *Khadga Srushti* which contains 'Some People Laugh, Some People Cry'. Perceived by many as obscure and prosaic, for Sri Sri this poem was an important expression of his accumulated experience. The dynamic blend of progressivism and nationalism is abandoned in favour of a subversive surrealism. Influenced by Freudian analysis, Sri Sri experimented with automatic writing to foreground hidden aspects of reality. He dedicated this collection of poems to the 'Telugu man' (telugu wadiki). The broad collective agenda of the earlier work is narrowed down in search of a distinctive, regionally situated, alternative Indian identity. However, Sri Sri soon realized that a combination of the surrealistic and the progressive modes was ideologically impossible. He acknowledged that surrealism was at best an experiment and moved away from it in his later work. Notwithstanding its uneasy aesthetic, 'Some People Laugh, Some People Cry', through a dense deployment of allusions and imagery, skilfully renders a chaotic world populated by suicidal philanthropists, one-eyed pups and unfinished sagas. Its interior landscape defies the location of meaning, and formlessness becomes an important index of experience.

FORWARD MARCH

The waves are rolling
The bells are tolling
The voice of another world is calling
Another another another world
Is rolling tolling calling on
Forward march
Oh onward forge
Ahead ahead let's always surge.

We reel and roll
With a song in our soul
Our galloping hearts shall reach the goal
The choice is clear
The hour is near

The voice of another world is dear
Thrilled by the call
Of the waterfall
Of another world we march onward.
Our blood in floods
Shall drench all roads
We leap the deep and sweep all shores
Reshaping geography amain
Remaking history again
Nor deserts nor forests nor hills nor rivers
Our forward march shall halt or reverse
East and west and north and south.

Eagles and lions and hounds of youth
Attack the turrets of humbug and hoax
The conservative the orthodox
Shall go to the wall shall come to the dock
Rottenmarrowed
Senile timeharrowed
Haggard laggards shall die on the spot
And shot by shot
Freedom's zealots
Proud heirs of tomorrow's thought
Their drizzling blood dazzling red hot
With shouts of 'Om
Harom Harom'.

Storm the bastile Reaction's home
And surge forward
Converge skyward
Lo another world a grander world
The banner of liberty has unfurled.

Forward march
Oh onward surge
Ahead ahead let's always forge
Bursting like cyclonic wind
Speedier than arrows or the speed of the mind
Blasting like the rainclouds' thunder

Yonder yonder yonder yonder
Lo the splendour lo the wonder
Of the burning 'Treta' light
Of another world lo there in sight.

Leapleapleaping
Eighty mighty
Million Meru mountains roar
Whirlwhirlwhirling
Doomgloombooming
Tidal waves of oceans roll
Youthful blood ignites the future
Youth awake is on the march
Towers of new life for to catch
Is this oil boiling? oh no
This is a lake of blood aglow
Like 'Niagara' like 'Nyanza'
Like resistless waterfalls
Bounce forward
Advance onward
Announce the birth of another world
Hear ye not the ringing singing
Drum beatings of another world?

Hail comrades denounce the useless
Dust and dirt of an age gone by
See before us rise the glorious
Mankind's hopelit spire of fire
Come like serpents
Come like greyhounds
Like 'Dhananjaya' claim the world
Hail the morn.
And sound the horn
A newer truer world shall be born
Then sing in chorus
Lo before us there is there is another world
Yonder yonder
Lo the splendour
And the wonder

Of its faery fiery crown
And the red flag of its dawn
Like the ritual flame of time.

Translated from the Telugu by the poet

FROM 'SOME PEOPLE LAUGH, SOME PEOPLE CRY'

(a prose poem)

A man walks on the bridge and gives away the change in his pocket to a beggar. He gives away his wristwatch to a nurse who happens to walk towards him. He throws his coat into the river and follows the coat into the water.

A man knows all the ins and outs of his trade. Rupee trees sprout in his palm. They lay golden eggs in banks. Tears drip from them like yolk.

A man sits silently near a milestone. He waits as if someone may arrive any minute. He eats peas as he counts buses. He forgets all time looking at a cloud.

A man wanders about carrying ladders—he has goose eggs in his bag. He leans his ladder against a wall. He climbs the ladder and throws an egg up into the sky. He is the same guy who bought Harishchandra for a heap of gold that high.

A man investigates holes. They differ in size.

A man offers anarchy for sale. He appears to be wading in space, searching for something with his long arms. He eats nothing but the giant lemon found in the lakes of blood in the hearts of the young. That too, only once a day.

A man spends time singing Raga Khamboji. It is not unnecessary to remind you that he has a lute with him. He has fingers only to legislate the ragas sung at appropriate times. At their touch stars catch fire. Lakes on the moon come to a boil. Winter begins to bud and my heart begins to offer marriage to the butterfly. A man puts camphor in his eyes and red lead on his cheeks. He is a poet. He interprets the messages he receives in secret code and works for the air force. He is the one big reason for the fall of prices in the market.

A man meditates with a string of *rudraksha* beads around his neck. What's the use of your knowing that there's no use in my pleading with people not to break coconuts in front of him?

A man loves only one woman. She dies. Follow the rest of the story on the silver screen.

A man gets hanged. Society buys peace with his death. The law sighs with relief. Every evening a blind dog visits the spot where his blood was spilled and barks piteously. This man was so proud he refused to say he was unjustly hanged.

A man becomes great by making speeches. Another becomes poor by drinking too much. One takes a copper from his maternal aunt and buys a kite. Another grabs it from him.

A man runs away. Another screws up his life. Another gets married. One man sleeps. Another dozes. Another talks and talks to while away time. One man's crying makes you laugh; another's laugh makes you cry. I can prove this with examples....

And on andonandonandonandonandon....

Sir, when will this end? Son, this is endless.

Translated from the Telugu by V. Narayana Rao and A. K. Ramanujan

ANNOTATIONS

'Forward March'

Title: The Telugu title is 'Mahaprasthanam'; literally, the great departure. While in the *Mahabharata* it refers to the spiritual journey undertaken by the Pandavas, here Sri Sri implores the people to march forward into the new world.

Lines 1–2
The references to the waves and the tolling bells are worked into the English version to recreate the taut onomatopoeic effect of the Telugu original and to foreground the immediacy of revolution.

Line 38
Harom: Hara + om. The poem's pervasive use of imagery associated with Siva, the Destroyer, anticipates the conclusion where the serpent—coiled around Siva's neck in traditional iconography—is seen as a symbol of power and an agent of change.

Line 39
bastile: Bastille, a fortress which was stormed by a mob of Parisians on 14 July 1789 to sieze its ammunition. Its demolition was inspired by working class anger against absolutism and marked the beginning of the French Revolution.

Line 47
cyclonic wind: Appears as 'sivasamudramu'—literally, Siva's ocean—and conjures up a vision of massive upheaval. Siva's *tandava nritya* could make the oceans churn and bring the world to the verge of destruction.

Line 52
'Treta' light: From *tretagni* or the three sacred fires of vedic ritual. 'The poet [Sri Sri] appears to elevate the fire of revolution to the religious fire of three-fold significance which dispels economic, moral and spiritual darkness.' *(Encyclopaedia of Indian Literature,* vol. 5, 1992, p. 4174.) The *treta yuga* is the second of the four *yugas (krita, treta, dwapara* and *kaliyuga)*— the time when Ramarajya existed. This is one of the many instances in the poem where Sri Sri combines myth with a modernist sensibility.

Line 56
Meru: The mythical golden mountain in the Himalayas, considered to be the axis of the universe and the abode of the gods. According to tradition, in primordial times when divine knowledge was accessible to all, it represented the common spiritual centre for mankind. The poet's vision of the new world crystallizes into one of the *krita yuga,* or the Golden Age.

Line 65

Like 'Niagara' like 'Nyanza': This line echoes the combination of Niagara and nagaara—or drum—in the original. Nyanza is from Victoria-Nyanza or Lake Victoria, the second largest freshwater lake in the world and one of the chief sources of the river Nile. Niagara is the large waterfall on the US-Canada border famous for its immense breadth and volume. Niagara has been used as a symbol of revolutionary fervour. The first anthology of Telugu progressive verse was called *Niagara* (1944).

Line 78

'Dhananjaya': Another name for Arjuna in the *Mahabharata.* Also a famous serpent which served as a rope to bind the horses of Siva's chariot during the burning of the Tripuras. The Tripuras are the three cities built by Maya, made of gold, silver, and iron. They were gifted to Tarakaksha, Kamalaksha, and Vidyunmali, the *asuras* or the demons who had achieved immortality through a boon granted by Brahma. These *asuras* were torturing the *devas* or the gods, and therefore had to be destroyed by Siva.

Lines 84–9

The original poem in Telugu insistently has recourse to combinations such as pushing-treading, stirring-spreading, flying-filling, whose energy is irresistible. The conclusion of the Telugu original with a powerful dual image of the *erra bavuta* (red flag) and the *homajwalalu* (sacrificial fires) juxtaposes the hiss of the fire with the swirl of the flag *(dhaga-dhaga, niga-niga, bhuga-bhuga).* It constitutes, as it were, the crescendo of the poem.

From 'Some People Laugh, Some People Cry'

Title: It should be noted that the Telugu original has a Hindi title, *'Koi has raha hai, koi ro raha hai'*. Sri Sri had come to hear by chance at a carnival, a song, *'koi has raha hai. koi ro raha hai/ koi jag raha hai, koi so raha hai'* (Some people laugh, some people cry/ Some people are awake, some are asleep) which 'seemed to go on endlessly'. A similar Telugu song haunted him: 'Siva lord of the world dug three lakes/ two of them never fill up/ another never dries up/ then came three potters/ one had no eyes/ the other two no legs/ those three/ made three pots/ one had no rim/ the other no body.' Its defiance of logic and resistance to closure had a direct bearing on the writing of this poem. Sri Sri's own translation of the poem is titled 'Three Cheers for Man'. The tone is one of bitter irony rather than of humanistic celebration.

Line 14
Harishchandra: Legendary king of Ayodhya known for his generosity and integrity. To honour a promise made in a dream to the sage Viswamitra, he gifted his entire kingdom and sold his wife, his child, and then himself.

Line 20
Raga Khamboji: A raga in the Carnatic system of classical music.

Lines 20–8
This section echoes the work of the English poets David Gascoyne (b. 1916) and Dylan Thomas (1914–53) whose surrealist work Sri Sri greatly admired.

Lines 25–6
A man puts camphor... cheeks: Camphor is often added to *kaajal* for its purifying properties in Andhra. Widows who were not allowed to apply *kaajal* put camphor in their eyes in earlier times. Traditionally men also applied *kumkum* on their foreheads after bathing. Sri Sri's reference to camphor is therefore not unusual. *Sindooram* from the Telugu appears as 'red lead' in the translation. Sri Sri's translation reads, 'Cheers for the man whose eyes are bleeding, whose cheeks are burning'. The bleeding of the eyes and the burning of the cheeks take on added significance as mixed metaphors for the watering and the stinging sensation caused by camphor.

Line 29
rudraksha: 'A tree, the small, round red fruit of which is dried and used as a bead on a "rosary" for japa, the ritual act of remembering and quietly intoning a formula or a god's name; the bead is especially prized by worshippers of Siva who consider it "supremely holy".' (Dharwadker and Ramanujan,1994, pp. 209–10).

Lines 47–9
Sri Sri translates the last section of the poem thus: 'Andajabhimudanda dada dada dadandada danda who dandanda dadandadanda dada dandada dandada danda dandandada........./– But, will this never end?/-

No, this will never end.' This line is taken from a Telugu play, *Pratāparudriyamu* (The Tale of Pratapa Rudra, 1897), by Vedam Venkata Sastry (1853–1929). Sri Sri wrote in a note to his translation, 'Almost meaningless gibberish, which I lifted from a Telugu drama, Prataparudriyam, in which the Prime Minister Yugandhara, in simulated madness, recites this metrically faultless verse. Faultless did I say? The caesura is missing in the first line. Only the first two words Andajabhima have any meaning but what exactly it is, is anybody's guess.' However, in the poem, the lines indicate the breakdown of language and signify the loss of meaning in an endless round of existence. The introduction of classical metre in this 'prose poem' may be seen as an attempt by Sri Sri to impart a dialogic structure to the poem, in which 'modern' and 'classical' elements are put in play.

SUGGESTED READING

Dharwadker, Vinay, 'Modern Indian Poetry and its Contexts', in A. K. Ramanujan and Vinay Dharwadker eds, *The Oxford Anthology of Modern Indian Poetry,* New Delhi: Oxford University Press, 1994.

Lal, Mohan ed., *Encyclopaedia of Indian Literature,* vol. 5, New Delhi: Sahitya Akademi, 1992, pp. 4173–5.

Prasad, V. Mohan, ed., *This Tense Time: An Anthology of Modern Telugu Poetry (1915–80),* Vijayawada: New Directions, 1981.

Reddy, Ramana K. V., ed. with an introduction, *Sri Sri Miscellany: A Collection of English Writings,* Vijayawada: Sri Sri Shashtipurti Sangham Publication, 1970.

Sastry, K. Srinivasa, 'Sri Sri's "Mahaprasthanam": A Response', in *Indian Literature, 22,* no. 3 (1979), pp. 56–61.

Subbarayudu, G. K., and C. Vijayasree, 'Twentieth Century Telugu Literature', in Nalini Natarajan ed., *A Handbook of Twentieth Century Literatures of India,* Connecticut: Greenwood Press, 1996.

G. M. Muktibodh
(1917–64)

Gajanan Madhav Muktibodh was born in Sheopuri, near Gwalior, in Madhya Pradesh. He received his preliminary education at Ujjain and Indore and obtained his BA degree in 1938. After that he taught in various schools and evolved into a Marxist thinker and poet from the early forties. Muktibodh was a member of the Communist Party for a while and continued to be associated with it until his death. He ran study circles for teachers, writers, and women workers; founded the 'Madhya Bharat Pragatisheel Lekhak Sangh' (The Central India Progressive Writers' Association) in 1942; and organized a conference of writers who were opposed to fascism at Indore in 1943. Muktibodh moved to Nagpur in 1948 where he faced acute financial difficulties and wrote some of his best known poems. He worked for a while as a journalist in the Department of Information and Publication of the Madhya Pradesh Government, and then as editor in the regional news services division of All India Radio. However, his communist affiliations made it difficult for him to continue in government service. He therefore left his job to work as editor of the radical paper *Naya Khoon* (New Blood) for which he wrote several pieces on literary, political and economic affairs, championing the cause of labourers and exposing corruption. Muktibodh obtained his MA degree from Nagpur University in 1953 and was consequently able to get a lectureship at Digvijaya College, Rajnandgaon, in 1958. This was a period of comparative stability in his life, though it was marred by the ban imposed in 1962 by the Madhya Pradesh government on his *Bharat: Itihaas aur Sanskriti* (India: History and Culture), which had been prescribed as a textbook for Higher Secondary schools. The book was banned for its Marxist view of history and its criticism of some aspects of Hinduism and Jainism. This was a traumatic experience for

Muktibodh, and he thought that the campaign against his book was indicative of the rise of fascism. His long poem 'Andhere Mein' (In the Dark) articulates his apprehensions about the growing menace of fascism. Meanwhile, Muktibodh's health deteriorated and he died in 1964 after a protracted illness. The trajectory of his life was that of a revolutionary middle class poet who lived in penury practically all his life but who refused to compromise on his principles, no matter what the cost.

The influences on Muktibodh's poetry and thought were many and diverse: Premchand, who was his mother's favourite author; Marathi Literature; Rabindranath Tagore; Mahatma Gandhi; the French philosopher Henri Bergson; the psychologists Sigmund Freud and Carl Jung; French and Russian Literature, especially the humanism of Leo Tolstoy, the tortured sensibility of Fyodor Dostoevsky and the acute psychological analysis of Maxim Gorky; modernist poetry of the early twentieth century, notably that of T. S. Eliot; and surrealism. The predominant influence on Muktibodh was of course that of Marxism, although there are strains of existentialism and mysticism, too, in his work. He attempted creatively to develop Marxism in the sphere of aesthetics and believed that the political and the literary were inseparable. If the protagonist of 'Andhere Mein' is in search of the supreme expression, it is for the articulation of a revolutionary vision. Muktibodh believed that a writer's perspective should be international. Consequently, his political poems and writings reflect an entire age in their rendering of the struggle of humanity for equality and independence. They gain added force because they are informed by a knowledge of history, politics, and economics. Poems such as 'Andhere Mein' and 'Chambal Ki Ghati Mein' (In the Valley of Chambal) have a panoramic range and sweep, encompassing several ideological terrains and moments in time, in order to depict human beings caught in the web of history from which they struggle to find a way out. A major concern in Muktibodh's work is the role and predicament of the middle class and the relationship between the personal and the social. In his poem, 'Zindagi Burada To Barud Banegi Hi' (Life is Sawdust so it has to become Gunpowder) Muktibodh is critical of middle class writers and intellectuals who support the oppressed for their own ends but they hang on to the needles of the clock tower because they do not want history to move. According to Muktibodh, middle class individuals may be self-aware and sympathetic but they cannot protest because they are too caught up in their feelings of guilt. The protagonist in the poem 'Brahmarakshasa' (The Ghost of a Brahman) cannot attain liberation because he is imprisoned within his own consciousness, far removed from the struggles of the people. As Muktibodh emphasizes in 'Chambal Ki Ghati Mein', 'liberation can never be attained in solitude; if it is there at all, it is there together with everybody else'. The personae in the poems are often fragmented, but their internal conflicts are symptomatic of the conflicts in society. Muktibodh in fact often invites his readers to de-class themselves and exhorts them to take a political stand.

Muktibodh's poetry is experimental and deeply speculative. There is a complex interplay of reality and fantasy in his poems through the use of surrealistic images that juxtapose several levels of existence. These images powerfully evoke a mysterious strangeness and a sense of horror to dramatize the psychological turbulence of the protagonists. There is also a strong narrative element in many poems which gives them an epic dimension. Muktibodh plays with intricate patterns of the sound of Hindi words that are untranslatable. There are often several languages within a poem as well as transitions from the poetic to the unpoetic, as in T.S. Eliot's poetry. A wide range of perspectives can be seen in constant clash and antagonism in Muktibodh's creative and critical work, as in his poem, 'Andhere Mein'; in his novel, *Vipatra;* and in his criticism, *Ek Sahityik Ki Diary* (The Diary of a Litterateur) and *Nai Kavita Ka Atamsangharsh* (The Internal Conflict of the New Poetry). Besides these works, Muktibodh wrote *Kamayani: Ek Punarvichar* (1961), which is a reconsideration of Jaishankar Prasad's Hindi classic, *Kamayani;* two collections of short stories, *Satah Se Uthta Adami* (Man Rising from the Surface) and *Kaath Ka Sapna* (A Dream of Wood); and a collection of poems, *Chand Ka Munh Terha Hai* (The Face of the Moon is Crooked, 1964). Except for *Kamayani: Ek Punarvichar,* all these works were published posthumously. 'The Void' and 'So Very Far' are included in 'Chand Ka Munh Terha Hai'. 'The Void' is a surrealistic poem which powerfully evokes the horror, destruction and violence that result from extreme self-absorption and a sense of the meaninglessness of life. 'So Very Far' emphasizes the class divisions in society and the inability of the individual to bring about any significant social change.

THE VOID

The void inside us
has jaws,
those jaws have carnivorous teeth;
those teeth will chew you up,
those teeth will chew up everyone else.
The dearth inside
is our nature,
habitually angry,
in the dark hollow inside the jaws
there is a pond of blood.
This void is utterly black,
is barbaric, is naked,
disowned, debased,
completely self-absorbed.
I scatter it,
give it away,
with fiery words and deeds.
Those who cross my path
find this void
in the wounds
I inflict on them.
They let it grow,
spread it around,
scatter it and give it away
to others,
raising the children of emptiness.
The void is very durable,
it is fertile.
Everywhere it breeds
saws, daggers, sickles,
breeds carnivorous teeth.
That is why,
wherever you look,
there is dancing, jubilation,

death is now giving birth
to brand new children.
Everywhere
there are oversights
with the teeth of saws,
there are heavily armed mistakes:
the world looks at them
and walks on,
rubbing its hands.

Translated from the Hindi
by Vinay Dharwadker

SO VERY FAR

I am so very far from you people,
My fires are so very different from yours,
That what's poison for you is food for me.

Multitudes walk with me in my isolation;
In my loneliness, friendly hands
Of those you despise, but caught
By my troubled soul and held precious there.
And that's why you rain your blows on me
In public and in private.
(Leaves of our blood-stained epics fly
In our fight.)

I covered myself with failure's trash,
Finding heaps on the spiral staircase
Of corruption and cash,
And though I've gone straight
I'm still bitter in what I do, hate
The poison.
For whatever one has one wants something better,
To sweep the whole world clean you need a scavenger
And I'm not him.
And though someone inside me roars each day
That no work is unclean if the man be true,
The work's still grim.

Beyond the world and its end-products:
Refrigerators, vitamins, radiograms,
There's my famished daughter.
In her intestines a gnawing nothing,
In her lungs the shame of those who have nothing.

Only suffering imprisoned by the nothings is true,
All else is unreal, untrue, a delusion, deceit.
The only truth is
A sequence of grief.

I am the split-eared, the underground wretch
Correcting disorders.
Under your Chevrolets and Dodges I stretch,
Oil-covered, black,
Bowed by your orders.

Translated from the Hindi by Vishnu Khare and Adil Jussawalla

ANNOTATIONS

'The Void'

Title: The title is 'Shoonya' in Hindi. It plays upon the philosophical concept of the void as the emptiness which is also fullness, the nothing which is the ultimate reality. Because it is nothing in particular, the void has the possibility of being everything, and its realization is a means of attaining salvation. In his poem, 'Ek Aroop Shoonya Ke Prati' (To a Formless Void), Muktibodh mocks the veneration of the void: 'This light-destroying journey in the darkness of a limitless cipher is also great'. Muktibodh uses the concept of the void as negativism which generates violence and destruction.

Line 13
disowned: 'Viheen' in Hindi, which means empty, or deprived.

Line 24
give it away: This translates better as 'distribute it'.

'So Very Far'
Title: The Hindi title is 'Main Tum Logon Se Door Hoon' which literally translates as 'I am far from you people'.

Line 10
our blood-stained epics: The original has the singular form 'my'.

Line 19
scavenger: The figure of the lowly scavenger is here elevated to the status of a representative of history.

Line 20
And I'm not him: The persona's recognition of his inability to assume the role of a scavenger is more poignantly expressed in the original which may be translated as 'I am unable to be that scavenger'.

Line 33
split-eared: This should probably be 'slit-eared'. The Hindi word in the original is 'kanphata', which is a designation for a sect of yogis. It is possibly used here to emphasize the persona's sense of his difference from the rest of society. There is also a note of self-mockery, for though the persona is 'slit-eared' like the yogis, he remains an 'underground wretch'.

SUGGESTED READING

Ramakrishnan, E.V., '"The Unachieved Absolute Expression" and the Modernity of Muktibodh', in *Making it New: Modernism in Malayalam, Marathi and Hindi Poetry,* Shimla: Indian Institute of Advanced Study, 1995.

Sharma, S. S., 'Chand Ka Munh Terha Hai', in K. M. George ed., *Masterpieces of Indian Literature,* vol. 1, New Delhi: National Book Trust, 1997, pp. 401–4.

Nissim Ezekiel
(b. 1924)

Nissim Ezekiel was born in Bombay of Jewish (Bene-Israel) parents who were devoted to education. To this heritage he owes his own deep involvement in education. He has taught in a school, at college and at university. He studied at Wilson College, Bombay, and at Birkbeck College, London. His stay in England from 1948 to 1952 marked a watershed in his life and career. According to Ezekiel, 'philosophy, poverty and poetry' shared his basement room in England and that confluence of experiences left its mark on his poetry. Besides writing poetry for over half a century, Ezekiel has been copywriter, literary critic, art critic, playwright, director of plays, and professor of English at the University of Bombay. He is an active member of the Indian branch of the P.E.N. (Poets, Essayists, Novelists) Club, which was formed in the 1920s. He has also been editor of *The Indian P.E.N., Quest, Imprint* and *Poetry India.* As editor and critic Ezekiel has influenced the theory and practice of several younger poets, besides making his own pioneering creative contribution to Indian poetry in English. His *Latter-Day Psalms* was selected for the Sahitya Akademi Award in 1983 and he was awarded the Padma Shri in 1988. Ezekiel has published eight volumes of poetry including *A Time to Change* (1952), *The Unfinished Man* (1960), *The Exact Name* (1965), *Hymns in Darkness* (1976) and *Collected Poems* (1989).

Ezekiel's contribution to Indian poetry in English is important both for its quality and its variety. His early poetry has close affinities with the work of T. S. Eliot, W. H. Auden, Ezra Pound and Rainer Maria Rilke. Ezekiel's poetry renders the contemporary themes of alienation, spiritual emptiness, isolation, and fragmentation with humour, compassion and irony. He draws his images from the cities he has known intimately, Bombay and London, in order to explore the contemporary ethos. Ezekiel's poetry is distinguished by his conscious craftsmanship, his philosophical and introspective mode, and his unpretentious yet restrained conversational style. He is a pathbreaker in the use of modern speech inflections within the framework of formal verse patterning. The lilt of Indian speech cadences often found in Ezekiel's poetry is not simply a token measure to show his cultural immersion in his environment. The poet's rootedness in the Indian ethos is evident in his series of eight poems, 'Very Indian Poems in Indian English', which are included in *Hymns in Darkness.* As his poem 'In India' reveals, Ezekiel's India may be dark and wounded but he does not wish to exchange it for any other place.

Of the three poems of Ezekiel included here, 'Enterprise' from *The Unfinished Man* (1960) marks an early phase in the poet's self-exploratory oeuvre. The poem can perhaps be read as an autobiography of Ezekiel's literary experiences during his stay in England. Allusions to a 'pilgrimage', 'the call', prayer, and 'grace' suggest that this rite of passage must have been a powerful spiritual experience for the poet, involving frequent doubts and self-scrutiny. The poet-persona uses irony to come to terms with the ambivalence of his literary and cultural position vis-a-vis European poetry. The specific geographical and material nature of the journey is reinforced by words like 'sea' and 'soap', which provide clues to the poet's alienation in a foreign land. Yet the reader is unable to reach with ease the bedrock of actual impulses that underlie this poem.

'Night of the Scorpion' from *The Exact Name* (1965) is a much-anthologized poem which belongs to the middle phase of Ezekiel's writing. As in some of the other poems included in the volume, the ordinary and the commonplace are treated with a simplicity that draws out the latent human emotions of the situation, elevating and transmuting them into poetry. The poem is in free verse, and the narrative attains added piquancy through the use of a conversational tone combined with the rhythms of ritualistic chant and prayer.

'Goodbye Party for Miss Pushpa T. S.' from 'Very Indian Poems in Indian English' (1976) is written in the form of a farewell speech. Here Ezekiel parodies with good humour the frequently flawed usage of what is called Standard English. A hybrid form of the language colloquially referred to as 'Babu Angrezi' is used in the poem to render ironically the confused usage of English by the Indian middle class. The original impulse of the poem may not be very charitable, but as in his other 'Very Indian Poems in Indian English', the poet's obvious sympathy prevents the speaker from becoming a mere caricature. What this poem achieves in the context of more recent debates about Indian English is the release of English from its British cultural antecedents.

ENTERPRISE

It started as a pilgrimage,
Exalting minds and making all
The burdens light. The second stage
Explored but did not test the call.
The sun beat down to match our rage.

We stood it very well, I thought,
Observed and put down copious notes
On things the peasants sold and bought.
The way of serpents and of goats,
Three cities where a sage had taught.

But when the differences arose
On how to cross a desert patch,
We lost a friend whose stylish prose
Was quite the best of all our batch.
A shadow falls on us—and grows.

Another phase was reached when we
Were twice attacked, and lost our way.
A section claimed its liberty
To leave the group. I tried to pray.
Our leader said he smelt the sea.

We noticed nothing as we went,
A straggling crowd of little hope,
Ignoring what the thunder meant,

Deprived of common needs, like soap.
Some were broken, some merely bent.

When, finally, we reached the place,
We hardly knew why we were there.
The trip had darkened every face,
Our deeds were neither great nor rare.
Home is where we have to earn our grace.

NIGHT OF THE SCORPION

I remember the night my mother
was stung by a scorpion. Ten hours
of steady rain had driven him
to crawl beneath a sack of rice.

Parting with his poison—flash
of diabolic tail in the dark room-
he risked the rain again.
The peasants came like swarms of flies
and buzzed the Name of God a hundred times
to paralyse the Evil One.
With candles and with lanterns
throwing giant scorpion shadows
on the sun-baked walls
they searched for him: he was not found.
They clicked their tongues.
With every movement that the scorpion made
his poison moved in Mother's blood, they said.
May he sit still, they said.
May the sins of your previous birth
be burned away tonight, they said.
May your suffering decrease
the misfortunes of your next birth, they said.
May the sum of evil
balanced in this unreal world
against the sum of good
become diminished by your pain.
May the poison purify your flesh

of desire, and your spirit of ambition,
they said, and they sat around
on the floor with my mother in the centre,
the peace of understanding on each face.
More candles, more lanterns, more neighbours,
more insects, and the endless rain.
My mother twisted through and through
groaning on a mat.
My father, sceptic, rationalist,
trying every curse and blessing,
powder, mixture, herb and hybrid.
He even poured a little paraffin
upon the bitten toe and put a match to it.
I watched the flame feeding on my mother.
I watched the holy man perform his rites
to tame the poison with an incantation.
After twenty hours
it lost its sting.

My mother only said
Thank God the scorpion picked on me
and spared my children.

GOODBYE PARTY FOR MISS PUSHPA T. S.

Friends,
our dear sister
is departing for foreign
in two three days,
and
we are meeting today
to wish her bon voyage.

You are all knowing, friends,
what sweetness is in Miss Pushpa.
I don't mean only external sweetness
but internal sweetness.
Miss Pushpa is smiling and smiling
even for no reason
but simply because she is feeling.

Miss Pushpa is coming
from very high family.
Her father was renowned advocate
in Bulsar or Surat,
I am not remembering now which place.

Surat? Ah, yes,
once only I stayed in Surat
with family members
of my uncle's very old friend,
his wife was cooking nicely...
that was long time ago.

Coming back to Miss Pushpa
she is most popular lady
with men also and ladies also.
Whenever I asked her to do anything,
she was saying, 'Just now only
I will do it.' That is showing
good spirit. I am always
appreciating the good spirit.
Pushpa Miss is never saying no.
Whatever I or anybody is asking
she is always saying yes,
and today she is going
to improve her prospect,
and we are wishing her bon voyage.

Now I ask other speakers to speak,
and afterwards Miss Pushpa
will do summing up.

ANNOTATIONS

'Enterprise'

Title: 'Enterprise' is the second of ten poems written by Ezekiel in 1959 which comprise the collection, *The Unfinished Man.* The volume begins with an epigraph from W.B.Yeats's poem, 'A Dialogue of Self and Soul', of which the two last lines are:

The unfinished man and his pain
Brought face to face with his own clumsiness.

Borrowing the title of this collection from Yeats's poem, Ezekiel enters into a similar dialogue with himself.

Lines 1–5
pilgrimage: This is perhaps an allusion to Ezekiel's journey to England. The pilgrimage is both real and imagined. The poet-persona is accompanied by others who set out responding to 'the call', but there is a gradual diminishing of their fervour.

Line 7
copious notes: The phrase is used ironically to suggest immaturity as well as the lack of a proper perspective and focus among the 'pilgrims'.

Line 9
The way of serpents and of goats: This could be a reference to the superior knowledge of nature that the 'peasants' have.

Line 10
Three cities...taught: This is as obscure as it seems precise. The allusion may be to T. S. Eliot or to Ezra Pound, who dominated the literary scene of Europe in the early twentieth century. Critics of Ezekiel's poetry have glossed over the obscurity of this reference. However, to impose a specific locale and identity would perhaps be to limit the range of possible resonance.

Line 12
desert: The metaphor of a journey through a 'desert' has reverberations of Ezekiel's own Jewish faith. There is a possible allusion to the wanderings of the Israelites through the desert when they were driven out of Egypt by the Pharaoh. The second book of the Bible, Exodus (the Greek word for 'departure') describes this journey.

Line 23
what the thunder meant: 'what the thunder meant' has echoes of 'What the Thunder Said', the last section of T. S. Eliot's *The Waste Land* (1922) where the poet-persona invokes the Fable of the Thun-

der from the *Brihadaranyaka Upanishad* V, 2 to provide the moral imperatives of *'datta'* ('give'), *'dayadbvam'* ('be compassionate') and *'damyata'*('control yourselves'). In 'Enterprise' 'thunder' perhaps refers to each writer's private moment of inspiration.

'Night of the Scorpion'

Lines 1–7
I remember the night... risked the rain again: There is a complex play of memory here, involving past childhood images of heightened fear alongside a more adult understanding of the situational irony that turns the victim-scorpion into an aggressor and back again into a victim who is exiled from its erstwhile shelter. The poet uses the fear-ridden impressions of the child's sensitive mind which coalesce with received images and notions of evil and darkness.

Lines 18–31
May he sit still...face: In these lines the poet uses multiple perspectives and provides a variation of rhythm in order to make an all-inclusive statement about the human condition. The child's silent observation, the scorpion's aggression, and the peasants' primitive wisdom are counterpointed through shifting perspectives. The ritualistic incantation of the pious hopes and wishes of the peasants has the form, pattern and rhythm of a prayer ('May he sit still... May your suffering decrease... May the sum of evil... become diminished'). These incantations invoke well-entrenched ideas in Indian philosophy such as rebirth, karma (the idea that one has to reap the fruits of one's deeds in following births), and maya (the Vedantic concept of the natural universe as one vast illusion).

Lines 36–45
My father... lost its sting: There is a powerful use of parallelisms and contrasts in these lines in order to juxtapose the rationalism and materialism represented by the father with the beliefs and superstitions of the peasants.

'Goodbye Party to Miss Pushpa T. S.'

Title: This poem was written in 1967, soon after Ezekiel began his series of poems, 'Very Indian Poems in Indian English'.

Line 2
sister: The poet is ironical about the unselfconscious Indian usage of kinship terms like 'uncle', 'sister' and 'mother' to address even casual acquaintances.

Line 8
You are all knowing: There is a dig at the use of the present continuous tense in place of the simple present tense, which is characteristic of Indian English.

Line 30
Just now only: The poem continues to parody Indian English. Ending sentences with the word 'only' is a common form of expression among speakers of Indian English.

Line 38
improve her prospect: Note the replacement of 'prospects' with the singular 'prospect'. The speaker perhaps implies that Miss Pushpa T. S. will improve not only her professional but also her marriage prospects by travelling abroad.

SUGGESTED READING

Daruwalla, Keki N. ed, *Two Decades of Indian Poetry:1960–80,* Delhi: Vikas Publishing House, 1980.

Garman, Michael, 'Nissim Ezekiel: Pilgrimage and Myth', in M. K. Naik et al., ed., *Critical Essays on Indian Writing in English,* Dharwar: Karnatak University, 1967.

Karnani, Chetan, *Nissim Ezekiel,* New Delhi: Arnold Heinemann, 1974.

Taranath, Rajeev and Meena Belliappa, *The Poetry of Nissim Ezekiel,* Calcutta: Writers Workshop, 1966.

JAYANTA MAHAPATRA
(b. 1928)

Jayanta Mahapatra was born in Cuttack, Orissa, in a Christian family. He received his early education at Stewart European School. Later, he studied Physics at Ravenshaw College, Cuttack and at Patna Science College. He taught at various colleges in Orissa till his retirement. His father's job as sub-inspector of primary schools often kept him away from home. Indeed, he is the 'missing person' that Mahapatra writes about in a poem of the same title. Later on in life the father introduced the son to the 'yellowed diary' of the poet's grandfather that recorded the grandfather's conversion to Christianity in 1866 in order to escape death from starvation.

Mahapatra began writing poetry at the age of forty. His poems were first published abroad in journals like *Critical Quarterly,* the *Kenyon Review* and the *Sewanee Review.* He is the author of more than a dozen collections which include *Close the Sky, Ten by Ten* (1971), *A Rain of Rites* (1976), *Relationship* (1980), *Life Signs* (1983), *A Whiteness of Bone* (1992) and *Shadow Space* (1997). Mahapatra also writes in Oriya and translates frequently from Oriya literature. He has rendered into English the works of leading Oriya poets like Gangadhar Meher, Sachi Routray, Soubhagya Mishra and Sitakanta Mahapatra. He has edited *Chandrabhaga* (a literary journal), *Kavya Bharati,* and the poetry section of *The Telegraph.*

Mahapatra's poetry springs from deep personal experiences. In his prose and in his interviews Mahapatra often refers to his loneliness and separation from his father, to his family history, and to the 'vast... Hindu amphitheatre' surrounding him. As he once said,'... we grew up between two worlds. The first was the home where we were subjected to a rigid Christian upbringing... the other was the vast and dominant Hindu amphitheatre outside, with the preponderance of rites and festivals which represented the way of life of our own people.' Mahapatra's poetry constantly engages with the past and its loss through a sensitive recounting of events and episodes from the history of Orissa and through the multiple references to local myths, legends, rituals, traditional practices, and sites of religious and social significance. The poet uses images and symbols drawn from various sources, such as the elements of nature; the numerous temples and their ruins around the towns of Puri, Cuttack and Konarak in Orissa; animals; physical activities; and diseases. Unlike the poetry of Nissim Ezekiel who had begun writing much earlier, Mahapatra's poetry is suggestive rather than descriptive, implicit rather than explicit, local rather than national. For Mahapatra, individual identity is the chief negotiating factor in the exploration of an emotional response to reality. His own Oriya identity is of crucial importance to Mahapatra in articulating a local rather than a pan-Indian voice in Indian English poetry. As he has never tired of saying, he is 'an Oriya poet who incidentally writes in English'.

In 'Hunger' (1976), the dramatic narrative which unfolds in four taut stanzas is based on the privations of a poor fisherman who drives his young daughter into prostitution. Hunger for food merges with hunger for sex as the narrator-protagonist accepts the fisherman's offer of his daughter. 'Dhauli' (1979) is a sensitive account of the historical catastrophe of the Kalinga war that wiped out thousands of lives to satiate a single individual's lust for power and suzerainty. Mahapatra does not hail the power and the military exploits of Ashoka: his sympathy reaches out instead to the vanquished and the dead who find no mention in Ashoka's rock edicts. The poem is elegiac in tone and speculative in style. While in 'Dhauli' the poet deals with a large historical omission, in 'Grandfather' (1983), the disasters of the Orissa famine of 1866 are viewed from a biographical perspective. The poet relates the harrowing experience of his grandfather, Chintamani Mahapatra, who was compelled to embrace Christianity in order to save his life during the famine. This decision was a hard compromise as he was left with an unfair choice between death and conversion. Mahapatra tries to relive that critical moment of choice by retrieving his grandfather's diary and by asking him imaginary questions. This too is a poem about 'hunger' and what it might do to its victims. 'A Country' (1983) is one of Mahapatra's more overtly political poems in which he suggests that suffering is universal, no matter what the social or the political order may be.

HUNGER

It was hard to believe the flesh was heavy on my back.
The fisherman said: Will you have her, carelessly,
trailing his nets and his nerves, as though his words
sanctified the purpose with which he faced himself.
I saw his white bone thrash his eyes.

I followed him across the sprawling sands,
my mind thumping in the flesh's sling.
Hope lay perhaps in burning the house I lived in.
Silence gripped my sleeves; his body clawed at the froth
his old nets had only dragged up from the seas.

In the flickering dark his lean-to opened like a wound.
The wind was I, and the days and nights before.
Palm fronds scratched my skin. Inside the shack
an oil lamp splayed the hours bunched to those walls.
Over and over the sticky soot crossed the space of my
mind.

I heard him say: My daughter, she's just turned fifteen...
Feel her. I'll be back soon, your bus leaves at nine.
The sky fell on me, and a father's exhausted wile.
Long and lean, her years were cold as rubber.
She opened her wormy legs wide. I felt the hunger there,
the other one, the fish slithering, turning inside.

DHAULI

Afterwards
when the wars of Kalinga were over,
the fallow fields of Dhauli
hid the blood-split butchered bodies.
As the earth

burrowed into their dead hunger
with its merciless worms,
guided the foxes to their limp genitals.

Years later, the evening wind,
trembling the glazed waters of the River Daya,
keens in the rock edicts the vain word,
like the voiceless cicadas of night:

the measure of Asoka's suffering
does not appear enough.
The place of his pain peers lamentably
from among the pains of the dead.

GRANDFATHER

The yellowed diary's notes whisper in vernacular.
They sound the forgotten posture,
the cramped cry that forces me to hear that voice.
Now I stumble in your black-paged wake.

No uneasy stir of cloud
darkened the white skies of your day; the silence
of dust grazed in the long afternoon sun, ruling
the cracked fallow earth, ate into the laughter of your flesh.

For you it was the hardest question of all.
Dead, empty trees stood by the dragging river,
past your weakened body, flailing against your sleep.
You thought of the way the jackals moved, to move.

Did you hear the young tamarind leaves rustle
in the cold mean nights of your belly? Did you see
your own death? Watch it tear at your cries,
break them into fits of hard unnatural laughter?

How old were you? Hunted, you turned coward and ran,
the real animal in you plunging through your bone.
You left your family behind, the buried things,

the precious clod that praised the quality of a god.

The imperishable that swung your broken body,
turned it inside out? What did faith matter?
What Hindu world so ancient and true for you to hold?
Uneasily you dreamed toward the centre of your web.

The separate life let you survive, while perhaps
the one you left wept in the blur of your heart.
Now in a night of sleep and taunting rain
my son and I speak of that famine nameless as stone.

A conscience of years is between us. He is young.
The whirls of glory are breaking down for him before me.
Does he think of the past as a loss we have lived, our own?
Out of silence we look back now at what we do not know.

There is a dawn waiting beside us, whose signs
are a hundred-odd years away from you, Grandfather.
You are an invisible piece on a board
whose move has made our children grow, to know us,

carrying us deep where our voices lapse into silence.
We wish we knew you more.
We wish we knew what it was to be, against dying,
to know the dignity

that had to be earned dangerously,
your last chance that was blindly terrifying, so unfair.
We wish we had not to wake up with our smiles
in the middle of some social order.

A COUNTRY

It's the dust everywhere,
the burden on my eyes:
for they belong to Asia where the air
is burnt and incense and ash
pile up on their misty whites,

where a hunger keeps growing
from Turkey to Kampuchea,
and the years keep trying to smile
in the stubborn starvation light.

When darkness falls
the old speak of the past with sleepy voices;
my ears tremble when I hear their tales.
I look at their faces,
and their eyes are dead as stone.
Here is my world, and it makes me dream as a child;
yet why do I wear myself out
feeling for the girls who die
before their breasts are swollen with milk?

Why am I hurt still
by the look in the hand
of that graceful Naxal girl
who appeared out of nowhere that winter,
holding a knife as old as history?

Sometimes at night
when all voices die
my mind sees earth, my country—
to accept sacrifice, the loss of friends,
and sons who vanished
suddenly in 'seventy-two.
However much I provoke and curse
I am unable to force an answer out of you.
Wherever I try to live,
in pious penitence at Puri
or in the fiery violence of a revolutionary
my reason becomes a prejudiced sorrow
like socialism.

And not understanding myself,
not understanding you,
like the still, strange shapes of hills in the distance,
I, too, listen to the faraway wailing of hyenas

aware of the dying countryside around them,
tortured by hunger and the reek of decay in the air
after the age-old myths
have been told all over again.

ANNOTATIONS

'Hunger'

Line 1

the... back: The poet recognizes the sexual urge but also views it as 'heavy'. This method of combining the literal and the metaphorical has been repeated in phrases like 'trailing his nets and his nerves' (line 3), 'I saw his white bone thrash his eyes' (line 5), 'burning the house I lived in' (line 8), 'his lean-to opened like a wound' (line 11), and 'her years were cold as rubber' (line 19).

Line 5

his ... eyes: Here, 'white bone' implies emaciation and 'eyes' are suggestive of inner vision or conscience.

Line 7

sling: Because the 'act' is a burden on him.

Line 8

Hope... lived in: The house refers to the body. Burning is perhaps a reference both to the desire of the flesh and to the process of spiritual purification.

Line 16

I heard him say: Note the change from 'The fisherman said' in the second line to 'I heard him say' here. Perhaps the attempt is to foreground the narrative and to make the narrator-protagonist a passive agent in a situation of his own making.

'Dhauli'

Title: The poet refers to the calamitous consequences of the Kalinga war. The kingdom of Kalinga largely coincides with modern day Orissa. The historical Kalinga war was fought in 261 BC between the Mauryan king Ashoka and the ruler of Kalinga. Although Ashoka won the battle by completely routing the enemy force, it heralded a turning point in his life. After the battle, Ashoka decided to lay down arms in order to lead a life of piety and to propagate Buddhism. Dhauli was the battlefield of this significant war. Legend has it that the adjoining river, Daya, turned into a bloody stream with the slaughtered bodies of the warriors.

Line 1
Afterwards: The reference here is to the period immediately after the Kalinga war.

Lines 5–8
As... genitals: A powerful image based on the perception that martial conquest is an act of virility. What remains now of this 'great' victory, however, is the expended masculinity of the so-called triumphant soldiers. The image of the foxes gnawing at the limp genitals of the soldiers is a powerful evocation of the limitations of male sexual power.

Lines 11–12
keens... night: The Ashokan rock edicts that were subsequently installed in Dhauli elaborately describe the monarch's kindness and the benevolent measures that he adopted towards the cause of Dhamma (or Dharma). However, the edicts do not record any plea for forgiveness by the emperor for the mindless butchering and blood-bath. Like the 'voiceless cicadas' which do not convey anything significant, the Ashokan rock edicts, for all their glorification of the emperor, are rendered meaningless by the stark absence of any confession of guilt, let alone of repentance. The reference to the 'voiceless cicadas' heightens the irony, for cicadas are insects known for their prolonged, shrill notes.

'Grandfather'

Line 1
vernacular: The poet's grandfather had written his diary in Oriya.

Lines 23–4
What Hindu world...web: The poet reconstructs this imaginary debate in the mind of the grandfather. Ultimately, faith succumbs to the demands of the body.

Lines 43–4
We wish... social order: This may be a reference to some state-imposed social order which feeds people but at the cost of their dignity.

'A Country'

Line 7
Turkey to Kampuchea: Two widely separated Asian countries with diverse socio-political and economic orders.

Line 14
dead as stone: Bereft of hope; also a reference to the dead who had lost their lives in the struggle.

Lines 21–9
Naxal girl... 'seventy-two: This is a reference to the extreme Leftist Naxalite movement which was violently crushed in the early seventies in states like West Bengal.

Lines 33
pious penitence at Puri: Many Hindus go to the town of Puri, one of the chaturdhams or four holy sites, on a purificatory pilgrimage to visit the temple of Lord Jagannath at least once in their lives.

SUGGESTED READING

Alexander, Meena, 'Jayanta Mahapatra: A Poetry of Decreation', *Journal of Commonwealth Literature,* 18, no. 1 (1983).

Mahapatra, Jayanta, 'About "Hunger" and Myself, *Keynote,* no. 1 (March 1982).

———, 'The Inaudible Resonance in English Poetry in India', *The Literary Criterion,* 15, no.l (1980).

Paniker, K. Ayyappa, 'The Poetry of Jayanta Mahapatra', in Vasant A. Shahane and M. Sivaramakrishna eds, *Indian Poetry in English,* Delhi: Macmillan, 1980.

Perry, John Oliver, 'Neither Alien nor Post-modern: Jayanta Mahapatra's Poetry from India', *Kenyon Review,* 8 (Fall 1986).

II. Short Stories

PREMCHAND
(1880–1936)

One of the most important writers of fiction in Hindi and Urdu, Premchand (his real name was Dhanpat Rai) was born in Lamahi, a small village near Banaras in eastern Uttar Pradesh. After passing his Matriculation in 1898, Premchand joined government service as a school teacher in 1900. He was married at the age of sixteen, but finding the marriage to be incompatible, he defied social convention by remarrying a child widow in 1906. Meanwhile, he passed the teacher's training examination from Allahabad in 1904. It was only much later in life, in 1919, that he obtained his BA degree from Allahabad University.

Premchand could sense in the atmosphere of the day a growing antagonism towards British colonial power. The environment in which he grew up was marked by a severe exploitation of the peasantry by a tradition-bound landlord class. Mahatma Gandhi's non-cooperation movement also influenced him deeply, and in 1921 he resigned his government job in the Department of Education to register his protest against British colonial rule. He devoted the rest of his life to writing, editing and publishing. Premchand later became somewhat disillusioned with the Gandhian movement and moved closer to Marxist thought in the late 1920s. A few months before his death in 1936, he delivered his famous Presidential address, 'The Purpose of Literature', at the first convention of the Indian Progressive Writers' Association, in which he highlighted the active social role of the writer.

Initially, Premchand wrote in Urdu as Nawab Rai. In Hindi he is known solely as Premchand. He was a prolific writer, as is evident from the numerous essays, comments and reviews that he contributed to various newspapers and magazines. This was in addition to the large number of short stories (about three hundred, compiled in eight volumes under the title *Mansarovar);* about a dozen novels; and two plays. In his early creative phase Premchand criticized the conditions of colonized India in a collection of short stories in Urdu, *Soze Watan* (The Lament of the Country), which was published in 1908. It was banned immediately and copies of the book were confiscated. Premchand's best known novels such as *Rangabhumi (The World As an Arena;* 1925) and *Godan (The Gift of a Cow;* 1936) focus upon the plight of the peasantry in the early twentieth century with deep sympathy and understanding. *Nirmala* (1927) is his poignant exploration of the predicament of a young woman who is trapped in an incompatible marriage with a much older man. Premchand also translated fiction from Urdu and English into Hindi, besides editing two magazines, *Madhuri* and *Hans.* His range of interests was vast and included, for instance, Akbar's poetry, constitutional rule in Turkey, the role of Oliver Cromwell in seventeenth-century England, and French fiction. An output of this magnitude made him a household name during his lifetime.

Premchand evolved an expression and an idiom entirely his own. Few, if any, translations can do justice to the vivacity of his language which is simple, flexible and precise. His descriptions communicate the flavour of spoken Urdu, with a generous sprinkling of the folk idiom. However, Premchand shunned the use of dialect, preferring standardized Hindi with its base of Khari Boli, which Hindi has exclusively taken over from Urdu. This approach, he thought, would make his work accessible to the people of the whole of north and central India—his purpose being to reach out as a writer to the widest possible readership. A pillar of the Indian National Movement in the realm of culture and literature, Premchand continues to be a guiding spirit for purposive, socially committed writing.

The short story 'Panch-Parmeshwar' ('The Holy Panchayat' in the translation included here) was first published in 1916. India was then involved in the First World War as a colony of Britain. In this story, Premchand looks towards the village community for a set of administrative rules that would provide an alternative to the colonial system of governance by deftly using the mythical dimension of justice which is supposed to reside in the heart of every human being. The story focuses upon the natural agency of self-governance and distributive justice in a rural community. At a deeper level, it locates the subtle workings of human consciousness in a living social environment. However, although the rural community appears to be idealized in the story, the social landscape is fraught with tensions. For instance, the clash of interests between Jumman and his clients reveals the fissures and conflicts within this community. Then there is the complaint of the birds who find very little worth emulating in the behaviour of human beings. And finally, there is the question of whether the larger social problem, raised by the injustice done to a helpless old woman, has been resolved through the suggestion that God operates as a spirit behind the panchayat. The problem has been resolved specifically in the case of the old aunt mainly because Algu, the shy, hesitant individual, was forced to occupy the seat of justice. But would this have happened if such a person as Samjhu Sahu had occupied that seat? These tensions make 'The Holy Panchayat' an extremely complex story which raises more questions than it seems to have resolved. Some of these questions persist in rural India even today where scenes of violent clashes between groups occur with disturbing frequency. Present day occurrences in the villages of India can be seen in an embryonic form in 'The Holy Panchayat', suggesting that as far back as 1916, the story gave an indication of things to come.

THE HOLY PANCHAYAT

Jumman Sheikh and Algu Chowdhari enjoyed a deep friendship. They cultivated their lands jointly. They trusted each other implicitly. When Jumman went to Mecca for Haj, he left his house in charge of Algu, and whenever Algu went away from the village, he would leave his house with Jumman. They would not eat with each other, nor did they share the same religion, but they used to think alike. This is the true meaning of friendship.

This friendship was born when they were both children, and Jumman's respected father Jumrati used to teach them. Algu had attended to his teacher's personal needs and many times he had washed cups and saucers for him. He never allowed his teacher's *hukka* to get cold even for a minute, because each time he escaped to fill the *chillum,* he could avoid his books for half an hour. Algu's father was a man of old-fashioned ideas. He did not believe so much in formal education as in looking after the personal needs of the teacher. He would say that education is not derived only from reading books, but one learns more from the teacher's blessings. One only needed his teacher's benevolence. Therefore if there was no apparent benefit to Algu from Jumrati Sheikh's blessings or his good company, he would console himself with the thought that although he had worked hard for his education, if knowledge was not in his *kismet* what could he do?

But Jumman's father thought along different lines. He was not much interested in being a benevolent teacher. He had more faith in his stick, and he was worshipped in all the nearby villages because of his firmness. If he wrote out a document, even the court clerk dared not make a change. The postman, the constable, and the tehsil *chaprasi*—they all respected him. As such, if Algu's respect was because of his wealth, people respected Jumman for his wisdom and education.

Jumman Sheikh had an old aunt. She had a little property but no close relatives. After making many false promises, he had persuaded the old woman to transfer the property in his name. Till the papers were registered in court, he showered her with attention. He would bring her sumptuous food and sweets. But the final stamping of the transfer deed put an end to this glorious period. Jumman's wife Kariman's sharp tongue was now added as a curry along with the *roti.* Jumman also grew more cruel and indifferent. The poor aunt had to listen to a lot of unhappy talk every day. 'God knows how long the old woman will live! She imagines that by giving us three bighas of land, she has bought us! She is unable to chew her *roti* unless there is *ghee* in her *dal!* With the amount of money spent on feeding her, we could have bought the whole village.'

The aunt tolerated this kind of talk as long as she could, then she complained to Jumman. But Jumman felt it would be unwise to interfere in the functioning of the 'officer on duty'—the mistress of the house. Somehow things carried on like this for a few more days. At last one day the aunt said to Jumman, 'I don't think I can live with you any longer. Just give me a few rupees and I'll cook my own food.'

Jumman answered rudely, 'Does money grow on trees here?'

The aunt pointed out politely, 'My needs are very little, but I must make ends meet all the same.'

Jumman answered with great seriousness, 'I had no idea that you were determined to live for ever.'

The aunt was upset. She threatened to go to the village panchayat. Jumman laughed to himself like a hunter does, when he watches his prey walk towards the trap. 'Yes. Go to the panchayat. The matter must be settled. I too don't like these daily arguments.'

Jumman had no doubt who was going to win at the panchayat meeting. After all, who was there in all the nearby villages who was not obliged to Jumman in many ways. Who in the village possessed the courage to challenge him! It was not angels from heaven who were going to participate in the panchayat.

In the days to follow, the old aunt, a stick in her hand, went around from village to village. Her back was bent like a bow. Every step she took was painful. But a problem had come up; it was necessary to solve it.

The old woman poured out her lament to every good man who was willing to listen to her. Some tried to console her and put her off; others cursed the cruel times. They admonished her. 'You have one foot in the grave; here today and gone tomorrow. But you can't stop your greed. What are you after, woman? Just eat your *roti* and pray to God! What do you want with lands and crops?' There were some who found this amusing—bent back, sunken cheeks, white hair. There were very few who were law-abiding, kind and considerate, who listened attentively to the sad story and offered her consolation. In the end she reached Algu Chowdhari. She put down her stick, sat down, and rested.

'Son, you too must come to the panchayat meeting, if only for a few minutes.'

'There will be many others from the village who will be attending the panchayat. Why do you want me to go?'

'I have told my sad story to everybody,' She said, 'Now it is upto them to come or not.'

'I'll come along, but I won't open my mouth during the panchayat.'

'But why?' she asked.

'What answer can I give to this? It's my wish. Jumman is an old friend of mine and I can't afford to spoil my relationship with him.'

'Will you turn your back to justice for fear of ruining your friendship?'

We have a tendency not to bother about our religious traditions; we would even let them be destroyed. But we are always aroused when a challenge is thrown at our faces. Algu had no reply to her question, but her words kept resounding in his mind—will you turn your back to justice for fear of ruining your friendship?

The panchayat met under a tree in the evening. Sheikh jumman had already spread coverings on the earthen floor. He had also arranged for *paan, ilaychi, hukka* and tobacco for the panchayat members. Of course, he himself was sitting some distance away from Algu Chowdhari, and whenever anybody arrived at the meeting, he would greet them warmly. When the sun had set and the birds had settled down to their own noisy meeting on the tree, the panchayat started. Every inch of the sitting area was packed, but most people were only spectators. Among the invitees, only those came who wanted a favour from Jumman. A small fire had been lit in one corner and the barber was hurriedly filling chillums. It was difficult to tell whether there was more smoke coming from the smouldering dungcakes or from the puffing chillums. The boys were running around here and there. Some were fighting and abusing one another, while others were crying. The village dogs, thinking that there was going to be a feast, had collected in hordes.

The panchayat sat down. The old aunt appealed to them.

'Members of the panchayat! Three years ago I transferred all my property to the name of my nephew. All of you know this. In return for this, Jumman had agreed to feed and clothe me. Somehow, for a year, I managed to suffer through, but now I cannot bear their ill-treatment. I neither got enough food nor adequate clothes. I am a poor helpless widow, unable to fight in a court or durbar. Except for you all, who else will listen to my grief? I am willing to accept whatever you decide. If you think I am at fault, you can punish me. If you find Jumman guilty, explain matters to him. Why does he want to suffer a helpless widow's curse? I will be happy to abide by your decision.'

Ramdhan Misra, whose many clients had been given shelter by

Jumman in the village, said, 'Jumman Mian, better settle with the old woman now. Otherwise whatever the panch decide, you will have to accept. Or name your own panch.'

Jumman noticed that most of the panch members were people who were obliged to him in one way or another. He said, 'I will accept the panch's decision as the decision of God. Let my aunt select them. I have no objection.'

The aunt shouted, 'You creature of God! Why don't you come out with the names so that I should also know?'

Jumman replied angrily, 'Don't force me to open my mouth. It's your problem. Name whoever you want.'

The aunt realized that Jumman was trying to put all the blame on her. She said, 'Son, you should fear God! The panch is nobody's friend or enemy. What kind of talk is this? If you can't trust anybody, then let it go. I am sure at least you trust Algu Chowdhari. I will propose his name as the head panch.'

Jumman Sheikh was overjoyed, but he hid his feelings. In a calm voice he said, 'Whether you select Algu or Ramdhan it makes no difference to me.'

Algu did not want to get involved in their quarrel. He tried to back out. 'Aunt,' he said, 'Jumman and I share a deep friendship.'

The aunt replied in a sober voice, 'No one will turn his back to justice for the sake of a friendship. God resides in the heart of a panch. They speak in God's voice.'

Algu Chowdhari's nomination was accepted. Unhappy with her selection the opponents of Ramdhan Misra and Jumman silently cursed the old woman.

Algu Chowdhari said, 'Sheikh Jumman! You and I are old friends. Whenever the need arose, we helped each other. But at this moment, you and your old aunt are both equal in my eyes. Now you can make your statement to the panch.'

Jumman was confident that he had won the round and that Algu was talking for effect. So he said peacefully, 'Dear members! Three years ago my aunt transferred her property to me. In return I had agreed to look after her needs, and as God is my witness, I have caused her no trouble till today. I treat her as my own mother, as it is my duty to look after her. But there is always friction between the women in a household. How can I be blamed for that? My aunt wants a separate monthly allowance from me. You all know how much property there was. There is not enough income from it to pay her a monthly allowance. Apart from this, there is no mention of any monthly allowance in our agreement, otherwise I wouldn't have taken on this unnecessary headache. That is all that I have to say. The panch is welcome to decide as it wishes.'

Algu Chowdhari used to visit the courts frequently. So he knew a great deal about law. He began to cross-examine Jumman. Each question hit Jumman like a blow to the heart. Ramdhan was amazed at the skilful questioning. Jumman was wondering what had happened to Algu. Only a little while ago he was talking so differently. Was their old friendship going to prove of no use? Jumman Sheikh was lost in such thoughts when Algu announced the decision: 'Jumman Sheikh! The panches have considered the matter. It seems to them that the aunt should be paid a monthly allowance. It is our opinion that there is enough income from her property to pay her such an allowance. This is our decision. If Jumman is unwilling to pay her the allowance, the agreement should be cancelled.'

Jumman was stunned. His own friend! Who would have thought he would behave like an enemy and stab him in the back. It is in such situations as this that one comes to recognize one's genuine friends from false ones. What a trick of fate! Being let down by the very man he trusted most! This is called a friendship of evil times. People are deceitful and double-faced; that is why they have to face so much suffering. Diseases like cholera and plague are a punishment for their evil deeds.

But Ramdhan and other members of the panch were openly praising the just decision. This was the true panchayat. Friendship is all very well, but it must be kept in its proper place. Man's primary duty is to be just and true. It is the righteous who support the world. Otherwise it would have perished long ago.

This decision shook the foundations of the friendship between Algu and Jumman. Now they were not seen talking with each other. Their old friendship which had stood firm like a tree could not withstand the first blast of truth. Truly, that tree had been planted in sand. Now when they met, they were formal with each other. They greeted each other coldly as a sword greets a shield.

Algu's betrayal played on Jumman's mind all the time. He lived now only to take revenge.

It takes a long time for the results of a good deed to show, but the results of an evil deed can be seen at once. Jumman did not have to wait long for his revenge. The previous year Algu Chowdhari had bought a pair of beautiful, long-horned oxen from Batesar. For months people came from neighbouring villages to admire them. Unfortunately, a month after the panchayat decision, one of the oxen died. Jumman told his friends, 'This is the punishment for treachery. Human beings can act in whatever way they like, but God sees the good and bad behind one's deeds.' Algu suspected that Jumman had poisoned the ox. His wife also blamed Jumman for the mishap. One day she and Jumman's wife had a violent argument about it. All sorts of hateful, rude and sarcastic words were exchanged. Somehow Jumman managed to quieten the warring sides. He scolded his wife and persuaded her to come away from the battlefield. On the other side, Algu quietened his wife by using a stick.

One ox is of no use to a farmer. Algu searched for a matching ox, but could not find one. He finally decided to sell the animal. The trader, Samjhu Sahu, in the village, drove an ox-cart. He used to take *gur* and *ghee* to the market and return with salt and oil which he sold to the villagers. He thought if he could lay his hands on the ox, he could make three trips to the market daily, instead of one. He inspected the ox, took it on a trial run, and then after some haggling brought it home and tied it in his courtyard. He promised to pay for it within a month. Algu was so anxious to get rid of the ox that he did not mind if the money came in later.

With a new ox, Samjhu put on the pressure. He started making three, even four trips in a day. He was careless with the food and water for the animal, nor did he give it proper rest. At the market place, he would throw some dry straw before it. The poor animal had barely rested, before he was tied up to the cart again.

At Algu's house, the ox had been looked after well, with fresh water to drink. Apart from fodder, it was given grain and even a touch of *ghee.* Morning and evening it was cleaned and massaged. Its comfortable past had given way to a life of torture. It became half its size and its bones stuck out. The very sight of the cart filled it with dread. Every step it took was difficult. And since it was a pedigree ox, it could not tolerate being beaten.

One day, while making his fourth trip, Samjhu overloaded the cart. The poor animal was tired after the long day—it could barely lift its feet. Samjhu began to whip it and it began to run. After a few yards it paused to rest, but Samjhu was in a hurry and he began to beat the animal mercilessly. The poor ox again tried to pull the cart, but its strength failed and it collapsed on the ground. This time it was unable to get up. Samjhu beat it again and again, pulled its leg, pushed some sticks up its nose, but to no effect. Dead animals do not rise. Samjhu now grew really worried. He looked at the ox carefully, then loosened it from the cart. He didn't know how to get the cart to his house. He shouted and yelled, but there was no one around. There was also no village nearby. He hit the dead animal a few times, complaining, 'If you had to die, why didn't you wait till you reached home. Now who will pull the cart?'

The cart had been loaded with several tins of *ghee,* some of which had been sold and two hundred and fifty rupees from the sales were tied in his waistband. Apart from this were loaded bags of salt which he could not leave unguarded. In the end he decided to spend the night in the cart. He puffed at his *hukka,* sang a song, smoked again and kept trying to keep awake. But ultimately he dozed off. When he woke in the morning, he found his money gone along with several tins of oil. He beat his head with sorrow and wept. He reached home in a state of shock. When his wife heard the bad news, she cried and started abusing Algu Chowdhari. 'That mean fellow! His unlucky ox has ruined us! All our life-long savings have been stolen!'

Several months went by. Whenever Algu demanded the price of the ox, Samjhu would reply nastily, 'Here we have lost our life savings and you want money for the ox! You cheated me! You gave me a sick ox! You expect me to pay you? Do you take me for such a fool? I come from a trading family and I am not going to let you fool me. Go and wash your face in a dirty pit and then come and demand money from me. Okay, if you don't agree with this suggestion, then you can borrow my bull and plough your land. What more can you want?'

Algu had no shortage of enemies. At such times they would collect and side with Samjhu. But it was not easy to forego one hundred and fifty rupees. One day he too lost his temper. Samjhu's wife entered the fray. Samjhu picked up a stick. The argument turned violent. On hearing the commotion, people gathered around. They tried to pacify them. Finally the villagers suggested that the matter be decided in a panchayat, and both Samjhu and Algu agreed.

Preparations for the panchayat began. Both the men went about lining up their supporters. On the third day, the panchayat sat under the same tree. It was evening. In the field some crows were having their own panchayat. Their topic of discussion was whether they had any right over the peas growing in the fields. And until the matter was resolved, they felt they had every right to disapprove the chowkidar's loud yells as he went about guarding the fields. A group of parrots sitting on the branches of some trees had raised the question of how men could call them dishonest when they themselves did not hesitate to deceive their friends.

The panchayat sat down. Ramdhan Misra asked, 'Now what is the delay? Let us select the members. Well, Chowdhari, whom do you nominate?'

Algu said very politely. 'Let Samjhu choose them.'

Samjhu stood up and barked, 'I propose Jumman Sheikh.'

Hearing this, Algu's heart began to beat fast, as if someone had slapped him. Ramdhan was Algu's friend. He understood. He said, 'Chowdhari, do you have any objections?'

Resignedly, Chowdhari answered, 'No I have none.'

The knowledge of one's responsibility helps to improve our relationship with others. Whenever we behave badly, this inner realization helps to bring us back to the right path.

Cloistered in his comfortable cabin the newspaper editor will make scathing attacks on politics and ministers. But if by chance he were to enter politics, his style of writing changes and he becomes impartial, discriminate and very objective. This change comes about from the realization of his responsibility. In the same way, young people can be high strung, thoughtless, and temperamental. Their parents are afraid they might end up giving a bad reputation to the family. But when a young man has to shoulder the responsibility of his own family, he learns to be patient. This change comes about because of his own inner realization.

As soon as Jumman Sheikh was appointed sarpanch, he felt a

similar sense of responsibility for his high position. He thought, 'I am sitting on the highest throne of justice and *dharam.* Whatever comes from my lips will be treated with the same respect as the words of God. I must not stray even an inch from the truth.'

The panches began to question both the factions. For a long time, both sides and their supporters argued back and forth. They all agreed that Samjhu should make payment for the ox. But two of the men favoured the idea that Samjhu should also be compensated for the loss of the animal. Others insisted Samjhu should be punished to set an example to other villagers not to treat their animals with such cruelty. Finally Jumman announced the decision.

'Algu Chowdhari and Samjhu Sahu, the members have considered your case very thoroughly. It is only proper that Samjhu should pay the full amount for the ox. When he bought the ox, it was in good health. If he had paid cash down at the time, the present situation would not have arisen. The ox died because it was made to work very hard, and it was not fed or looked after properly.'

Ramdhan Misra spoke, 'Samjhu has deliberately killed the animal, and he should be punished for it.'

Jumman said, 'That is a different matter. We have nothing to do with that.'

Jhagru Sahu pleaded, 'Samjhu should not be treated so harshly.'

Jumman said, 'That is up to Algu Chowdhari. If he wants to give a concession, it will be because of his own goodness.'

Algu was delighted. He stood up and shouted, 'God bless the *sarpanch.*'

The entire crowd joined in 'God bless the *sarpanch.*' Everyone praised the decision. This is not the work of man; God lives in the heart of a panch. This was His blessing. Before the panch, falsehood will be swept away.

After a little while, Jumman came to Algu and embraced him. Said he, 'My brother! Ever since you became *sarpanch* and decided the case against me, I have been your deadly enemy. But today I learnt as a panch that I am neither anybody's friend nor anybody's foe. A panch cannot see anything except justice. Today I am convinced that God speaks through a panch's lips.'

Algu began to cry. His tears washed away the misunderstandings that had accumulated in their hearts.

Translated from the Hindi
by Rashme Sehgal

ANNOTATIONS

Page 55

'The Holy Panchayat': The original title is 'Panch-Parmeshwar'. The Panch are village-level legislators as well as judges acceptable to the contending parties in a feud. One of the contenders may propose the name of a judge in a specific case. Literally, the word 'panch' means five. The phrase 'Panch-Parmeshwar' projects the panch as an expression of the verdict of God.
Mecca for Haj: Muslims go on Haj or a holy pilgrimage to Mecca. Mecca is the birthplace of the Prophet Muhammad (d. 632) in Arabia and the chief place of pilgrimage for Muslims. *had washed cups and saucers for him:* This has connotations of humour. It is assumed by the village-folk that the pupil attains knowledge by doing simple chores for the guru. *hukka and chillum:* A smoking device used mainly in villages, with the *hukka* as the long pipe passing through water and the *chillum* (an earthen pot with a hole at the bottom) containing burning coal or cow-dung cake to roast the tobacco. A distinctive aspect of *hukka* smoking is that it is enjoyed in company and is a symbol of social togetherness.

Page 56

he would console himself... could he do?: There is a confusion in the use of pronouns here. The sentence could be better translated thus: 'Algu's father would console himself with the thought that he had spared no pains whereby Algu could acquire knowledge. However, if knowledge was not in Algu's destiny how could he possibly have obtained it?'
kismet: 'Bhagya' in the original. Destiny; one's lot.
a benevolent teacher: An orthodox, saintly teacher who imparts education to pupils through example and not precept.

and be was worshipped... firmness: This could read: 'and it was because of the power of that stick that Jumman was now worshipped in the nearby villages'.
tehsil chaprasi: A peon at a court in a tehsil, which is a division of a district.
Jumman Sheikh had an old aunt: The Hindi text, which has eight divisions, has a break in time here as the first section comes to a close and the second one begins.
He would... this glorious period: There is a sentence missing after this in the translation: 'It was as if the seal of the registry had also put a seal on this hospitality'.
Jumman's wife... indifferent: An alternative translation could be: 'Jumman's wife Kariman also started adding the hot, spicy curry of her sharp words to the rotis that she served'.
bigha: A measure of land equivalent to approximately five-eighths of an acre.

Page 57
The aunt pointed out politely...: The politeness has a touch of silent anger in the original as the aunt asks: 'Don't I need a few crumbs to subsist on?'
Jumman answered...: In the original, the interrogative form continues and is translated thus: 'Did anyone imagine that you have fought death to come here?'
In the days to follow...: The third section begins with this line.
There were some who found this amusing...: The amusement and sarcasm in Premchand's language are more evident when the comment is given in full: 'Some gentlemen found this to be a great source of entertainment. Bent back, sunken cheeks, hair like dry grass. Who would not have felt amused when there were so many ingredients to provide humour?'

Page 58
to justice: To justice and conscience.
The panchayat met under a tree in the. evening: The fourth section in the original begins with this line. From here onwards, the breaks have been shown as in the original Hindi text.
paan, ilaychi, hukka, tobacco: Together, these are offered to guests as a mark of welcome. *Paan:* The betel-leaf. *Ilaychi:* Cardamom. *You*

can punish me: This should read: 'You can give me a slap in the face'.
durbar: A royal court or hall of audience in which the nobility sits to watch the legal proceedings. In colloquial use a 'durbar' is the large assembly of favour-seeking individuals at an important person's place. As against the modern court in which the appointees of the government interpret and administer justice, a durbar is the court of a feudal ruler. Here, the use of the word lends irony to the situation. Since Jumman is an influential person in the village, the aunt fears that the panchayat might turn out to be his durbar.
Ramdhan Misra...own panch: This could be translated as: 'Jumman had given shelter to many of Ramdhan Misra's clients in his village. This was an affront to Ramdhan. He said, "Jumman Mian, whom do you elect as the panch? Decide that now. Afterwards you will have to abide by whatever they say"'.
Mian: Term of respectful or affectionate address for a man. Page 59
the opponents of Ramdhan Misra.. .the old woman: This is confusing. It should read: 'Ramdhan Misra and Jumman's other opponents silently cursed the old woman'.

Page 60
The panch is welcome to decide as it wishes: This refers to the members of the panchayat. A more apt translation would be: 'The panch are welcome to decide as they wish'. *This was the true panchayat:* In the original this is followed by the statement that the panchayat 'had clearly distinguished the milk in the water'. This refers to the mythical swan which, when offered a bowl of milk mixed with water, would drink only the milk and leave the water *(neer-kshir* in Sanskrit). In Indian mythology the swan traditionally represents a discriminating intelligence.

Page 61
Batesar: A place to the west of east Uttar Pradesh, known for the special breed of its oxen.
Algu quietened his wife by using a stick: 'Algu quietened his wife by using the proverbial argument of the stick' would be more appropriate.
Sahu: Petty trader and retailer in the village. *gur:* Jaggery.
Apart from fodder... bones stuck out: The description in the original is much more detailed and humorous. It translates thus: Tn contrast, at Algu's house, the flute of contentment would always

be playing. Our friend the ox was put in harness perhaps once in six months. He would playfully jump and run for miles on end. His daily meal would consist of fresh water, well-mixed arhar dal, and oil-cake with fodder. And not only this, occasionally he could also savour the taste of ghee. Morning and evening a man would give him a good massage on the back and pat him. Alas! over there comfort and contentment, and here, daily torture! In just a month he became worn out and his bones stuck out'.

Page 62
He shouted and yelled... no one around: A beautiful simile in the original has been omitted here. The sentence would translate thus: 'He shouted and yelled, but the narrow village-road closes like an infant's eye as soon as evening approaches. There was no one around'.
Go and wash your face in a dirty pit: 'Go wash your face in a pit first'. A typical Hindi expression which is used to convey the anger and determination of the speaker who has decided to refuse something to a person.
Samjhu picked up a stick: The author intends to point out the cowardly nature of the petty trader. The sentence should read: 'Samjhu quietly slipped away, perhaps to pick up a stick'. In villages, traders are objects of fun and ridicule for their supposed cowardice.

Page 63
discriminate: 'Discriminating'.

Page 64
dharam: Duty or social norm.
God bless the sarpanch: 'God bless the head panch'. However, Premchand uses the word 'Panch-Parmeshwar' which has been translated in the title as 'The Holy Panchayat'. The phrase in the original, 'Panch Parmeshwar ki jai', should therefore be translated as 'Long live the holy panchayat' and not as 'God bless the *sarpanch*'.

Page 65
His tears... their hearts: The last sentence of the story in the original which follows this has been omitted. It may be translated thus: 'The withered vine of friendship flourished once again'.

SUGGESTED READING

Gupta, P. C, *Literature and Society,* New Delhi: People's Publishing House, 1983.

Pandey, Geetanjali, *Between Two Worlds: An Intellectual Biography of Premchand,* New Delhi: Manohar, 1989.

Rai, Amrit, *Premchand: A Life,* translated from the Hindi by Harish Trivedi, New Delhi: People's Publishing House, 1982, rpt. New Delhi: Oxford University Press, 1991.

Swan, Robert O, *Munshi Premchand of Lamhi Village,* Durham, N.C.: Duke University Press, 1969.

R. K. Narayan
(b. 1906)

R. K. Narayan (Rasipuram Krishnaswami Iyer Narayanaswami Iyer), with Mulk Raj Anand and Raja Rao, belongs to the tertiary generation of the progeny of Macaulay's Minute—the English-educated intelligentsia in India. Born in a Tamil Iyer Brahmin family with a fetching background of English education: a maternal grandfather who was a venal revenue official nicknamed *kuthupatta* ('one who has been stabbed'), an uncle given to gin and meatballs, and-a disciplinarian father delighting in Carlyle and Pater on the one hand and, on the other, a maternal grandmother and a maternal uncle, both idealistic and energetic, engaged in social service, as well as a lively mother who was considered one of the best badminton players of her club in Mysore, though she played in her nine-yard sari. The child Narayan grew up, however, away from his parents and siblings, in Madras, under the tutelage not only of the idealist uncle but also of his dynamic maternal grandmother who gave him a valuable non-formal education which included an introduction to the various ragas of Carnatic music. A lonely child all the same, Narayan went to a Mission school in Madras until he rejoined his family in Mysore at the age of sixteen. The two years he spent failing to clear the University entrance examination turned out to be the second formative period in Narayan's life when he read voraciously and started writing. The third important phase followed the premature death (1939) of his wife Rajam whom he had married in defiance of custom, convention and dire astrological prognostication. During the critical period after her death he claimed to have acquired psychic powers and to have 'met' the discarnate spirit of his wife. He brought up his daughter Hema, their only child, and has not married again. Narayan shifted to Madras in 1990 to live with his daughter's family, but even Hema passed away prematurely in 1994. Today he claims that the time he spends with his great-grandchild is the best part of his day. Three statements sum up Narayan, the man and the writer:

'To be a good writer anywhere, you must have roots, both in religion and in family. . . . I have these things.'

'Religion is not a thing that anyone can openly avow—it's like one's underwear.'

'If I had to live again, I would want nothing different. I live from moment to moment. . . . Nothing really has gone wrong with me. I am deeply interested in life as a writer. That is perhaps why I have not gone mad.'

Narayan began writing at the age of eighteen. His early writing was in predictable imitation of the English Romantics, until in his mid-twenties, on a holiday in Visakhapatnam, he wrote his first short story in his now famous style of realism. Narayan started his first novel in an exercise book bought for him by his dynamic maternal grandmother, on Vijayadasami day in 1930. (The thirties were not only significant in the Indian socio-political scenario, they also happen to be the take-off decade for Indian writing in English). Then began another phase of Narayan's early struggle when he tried to publish in England. Finally, a friend took the manuscript of *Swami and Friends* to Graham Greene. They were both resident at the time in Oxford and were socialistically inclined in the perfervid thirties. '*Swami* to me is a book in ten thousand', Greene was to say later in a letter to Narayan. And on Greene's recommendation, the novel was published in 1935. Following its poor sales, the publisher turned down Narayan's second novel which, with Greene's intervention, was published by a different publisher. Because of its commercial failure, this publisher rejected the third novel which was then published, with a little more help from Greene, by a third publisher. Narayan got another break when he was first published in the United States in 1953. Narayan is a prolific writer with an extraordinary range. He has written over thirty books: novels, novellas, short stories, memoirs, travelogues, retold legends, causeries, columns, essays. With the daily discipline of self-faith, impelled by an instinct for nicely blending art with acumen, today Narayan is a 'best-seller' who has received several honours.

'The "M.C.C", a chapter taken from *Swami and Friends,* is offered here as a short story, which thus acquires a dual citizenship. Among the many virtues of *Swami and Friends* as a first novel, its unpretentiousness comes first. The very simplicity of the story indicates rare wisdom, thrifty talent, and daring originality of theme for an Indian writer in English. The novel establishes the character of Malgudi, with its hills and woods, its river and dirty lanes. The place grows through every novel that follows, but its essential character never alters—that of a 'small town located in a corner of South India'. The novel has a basic plan: 'a flight, an uprooting, a disturbance of order—followed by a return, a renewal, a restoration of normalcy' (K. R. Srinivasa Iyengar). Swami also establishes the sensitive *sattvic* temper, the conscionability, the restless truth-searching mind, the gentle sensibility which are the hallmarks of the Narayan hero of the early novels. Finally, the novel confirms what Greene considered to be the secret of Narayan's success: Narayan stakes everything on his creativity— his characters must live or the novel fails. As part of *Swami and Friends,* 'The "M.C.C."' integrates with the novel, thematically and structurally. As a piece of short fiction, 'The "M.C.C" offers a low-key drama of Indian childhood, both amusing and restrained, available to minds unspoilt by adult experience, and now identified with the art of R. K. Narayan.

THE 'M.C.C.'

Six weeks later Rajam came to Swaminathan's house to announce that he forgave him all his sins—starting with his political activities, to his new acquisition, the Board High School air, by which was meant a certain slowness and stupidity engendered by mental decay.

After making his exit from Albert Mission School in that theatrical manner (on the day following the strike), Swaminathan became so consistently stubborn that a few days later his father took him to the Board School and admitted him there. At first Swaminathan was rather uncertain of his happiness in the new school. But he excited the curiosity that all new-comers do, and found himself to his great satisfaction the centre of attraction in Second C. All his new class-mates, remarkably new faces, often clustered round him to see him and hear him talk. He had not yet picked the few that he would have liked to call his chums. He still believed that his Albert Mission set was intact, though, since the reopening in June, the set was not what it had been before. Sankar disappeared, and people said that his father had been transferred; Somu was not promoted, and that meant he was automatically excluded from the group, the law being inexorable in that respect; the Pea was promoted, but he returned to the class exactly three months late, and he was quite full up with medical certificates, explanations, and exemptions. He was a man of a hundred worries now, and passed his old friends like a stranger. Only Rajam and Mani were still intact as far as Swaminathan was concerned. Mani saw him every day. But Rajam had not spoken to him since the day when his political doings became known.

And now this afternoon Swaminathan was sitting in a dark corner of the house trying to make a camera with a cardboard box and a spectacle lens. In his effort to fix the lens in the hole that was one round too large, he was on the point of losing his temper, when he heard a familiar voice calling him. He ran to the door.

'Hallo! Hallo! Rajam,' he cried, 'why didn't you tell me you were coming?'

'What is the thing in your hand?' Rajam asked.

'Oh,' Swaminathan said, blushing.

'Come, come, let us have a look at it.'

'Oh, it is nothing,' Swaminathan said, giving him the box.

As Rajam kept gazing at the world through the hole in the cardboard box Swaminathan said, 'Akbar Ali of our class has made a marvellous camera.'

'Has he? What does he do with it?'

'He has taken a lot of photos with it.'

'Indeed! Photos of what?'

'He hasn't yet shown them to me, but they are probably photos of houses, people, and trees.'

Rajam sat down on the door-step and asked, 'And who is this Akbar Ali?'

'He is a nice Mohammedan, belongs to our class.'

'In the Board High School?' There was just a suspicion of a sneer in his tone. Swaminathan preferred to ignore this question and continued, 'He has a bicycle. He is a very fine Mohammedan, calls Mohammed of Gazni and Aurangazeb rascals.'

'What makes you think that they were that?'

'Didn't they destroy our temples and torture the Hindus? Have you forgotten the Somnathpur God?...'

'We brahmins deserve that and more,' said Rajam. 'In our house my father does not care for New-Moon days and there are no Annual Ceremonies for the dead.' He was in a debating mood, and Swaminathan realized it and remained silent. Rajam said, 'I tell you what, it is your Board High School that has given you this mentality.'

Swaminathan felt that the safest course would be to agree with him. 'You are right in a way. I don't like the Board High School.' 'Then why did you go and join it?'

'I could not help it. You saw how beastly our Head Master was. If you had been in my place, you would have kicked him in the face.'

This piece of flattery did not soothe Rajam, 'If I were you I would have kept clear of all your dirty politics and strikes.' His father was a Government servant, and hence his family was anti-political.

Swaminathan said, 'You are right. I should have remained at home on the day of the strike.' This example of absolute sub-mis-siveness touched Rajam. He said promptly that he was prepared to forgive Swaminathan his past sins and would not mind his belonging to the Board School. They were to be friends as of old. 'What would you say to a cricket team?' Rajam asked.

Swaminathan had not thought of cricket as something that he himself could play. He was, of course, familiar with Hobbs, Bradman, and Duleep, and vainly tried to carry their scores in his head, as Rajam did. He filched pictures of cricket players, as Rajam did, and pasted them in an album, though he secretly did not very much care for those pictures—there was something monotonous about them. He sometimes thought that the same picture was pasted in every page of the album.

'No, Rajam, I don't think I can play. I don't know how to play.'

'That is what everybody thinks,' said Rajam, 'I don't know how myself, though I collect pictures and scores.'

This was very pleasing to hear. Probably Hobbs too was shy and sceptical before he took the bat and swung it.

'We can challenge a lot of teams, including our School Eleven. They think they can't be beaten,' said Swaminathan.

'What! The Board School mugs think that! We shall thrash them. Oh, yes.'

'What shall we call it?'

'Don't you know? It is the M.C.C.,' said Rajam.

'That is Hobbs's team, isn't it? They may drag us before a court if we take their name.'

'Who says that? If we get into any trouble, I shall declare before the judge that M.C.C. stands for Malgudi Cricket Club.'

Swaminathan was a little disappointed. Though as M.C.C. it sounded imposing, the name was really a bit tame. 'I think we had better try some other name, Rajam.'

'What would you suggest?'

'Well-I am for "Friends Eleven".'

'Friends Eleven?'

'Or say "Jumping Stars"?' said Swaminathan.

'Oh, that is not bad, not bad you know.'

'I do think it would be glorious to call ourselves "Jumping Stars"!'

Rajam instantly had a vision of a newspaper report: 'The Jumping Stars soundly thrashed the Board High School Eleven.' 'It is a beauty, I think,' he cried, moved by the vision. He pulled out a piece of paper and a pencil, and said, 'Come on, Swami, repeat the names that come to your head. It would be better to have a long list to select from. We shall underline "Jumping Stars" and "M.C.C." and give them special consideration. Come on.'

Swaminathan remained thoughtful and started, '"Friends Eleven"...."Jumping Stars"...."Friends Union"____'

'I have "Friends Union" already here,' Rajam said, pointing to the list.

Swaminathan went on: '"Excelsiors". . . .'

'I have got it.'

'"Excelsior Union" . . . "Champion Eleven" . . . . ' A long pause.

'Are you dried up?' Rajam asked.

'No, if Mani were here, he would have suggested a few more names. . . . "Champion Eleven".'

'You have just said it.' '"Victory Union Eleven" . . . .'

'That is very good. I think it is very very good. People would be afraid of us.' He held the list before him and read the names with great satisfaction. He had struggled hard on the previous night to get a few names. But only 'Friends Union' and 'Excelsiors' kept coming till he felt fatigued. But what a lot of names Swaminathan was able to reel off. 'Can you meet me tomorrow evening, Swami? I shall get Mani down. Let us select a name.'

After a while Swaminathan asked, 'Look here, do you think we shall have to pay tax or something to the Government when we start the team?'

'The Government seems to tax everything in this world. My father's pay is about five hundred. But nearly two hundred and over is demanded by the Government. Anyway, what makes you think that we shall have to pay tax?'

'I mean—if we don't pay tax, the Government may not recognize our team or its name and a hundred other teams may take the same name. It might lead to all sorts of complications.'

'Suppose we have two names?' asked Rajam.

'It is not done.'

'I know a lot of teams that have two names. When I was in Bishop Waller's, we had a cricket team that we called—I don't remember the name now. I think we called it "Cricket Eleven" and "Waller's Cricket Eleven". You see, one name is for ordinary use and the other is for matches.'

'It is all very well for a rich team like your Waller's. But suppose the Government demands two taxes from us?'

Rajam realized at this point that the starting of a cricket team was the most complicated problem on earth. He had simply expected to gather a dozen fellows on the *maidan* next to his compound and play, and challenge the world. But here were endless troubles, starting with the name that must be unique, Government taxes, and so on. The Government did not seem to know where it ought to interfere and where not. He had a momentary sympathy for Gandhi; no wonder he was dead against the Government.

Swaminathan seemed to be an expert in thinking out difficulties. He said, 'Even if we want to pay, whom are we to pay the taxes to?' Certainly not to His Majesty or the Viceroy. Who was the Government? What if somebody should take the money and defraud them, somebody pretending to be the Government? Probably they would have to send the taxes by Money Order to the Governor! Well, that might be treason. And then what was the amount to be paid?

II

They sat round Rajam's table in his room. Mani held before him a catalogue of Messrs Binns, the Shop for Sports Goods. He read, '"Junior Willard Bats, Seven Eight, made of finest seasoned wood, used by Cambridge Junior Boys' Eleven".'

'Let me have a look at it . . . .' said Rajam. He bent over the table and said, 'Seems to be a fine bat. Have a look at it, Swami.' Swaminathan craned his neck and agreed that it was a fine bat, but he was indiscreet enough to say, 'It looks like any other bat in the catalogue.' Mani's left hand shot out and held his neck and pressed his face close to the picture of the bat: 'Why do you pretend to be a cricket player if you cannot see the difference between Junior Willard and other bats? You are not fit to be even a sweeper in our team.' After this admonition the hold was relaxed.

Rajam asked, 'Swami, do you know what the catalogue man calls the Junior Willard? It seems it is the Rolls-Royce among the junior bats. Don't you know the difference between the Rolls-Royce and other cars?'

Swaminathan replied haughtily, 'I never said I saw no difference between the Rolls-Royce and other cars.'

'What is the difference?' urged Rajam.

Mani laughed and teased, 'Come on. If you really know the difference, why don't you say it?'

Swaminathan said, 'The Rolls cost a lakh of rupees, while other cars cost about ten thousand; a Rolls has engines made of silver, while other cars have iron engines.'

'Oh, oh!' jeered Rajam.

'A Rolls never gives trouble, while other cars always give trouble; a Rolls engine never stops; a Rolls-Royce never makes a noise, while other cars always make a noise.'

'Why not deliver a lecture on the Rolls-Royce?' asked Mani.

'Swami, I am glad you know so much about the Rolls-Royce. I am at the same time ashamed to find you knowing so little about Willard Junior. We had about a dozen Willard Juniors when I was in Bishop Waller's. Oh! what bats! There are actual springs inside the bat, so that when you touch the ball it flies. There is fine silk cord wound round the handle. You don't know anything, and yet you talk! Show me another bat which has silk cord and springs like the Willard.'

There was a pause, and after that Rajam said, 'Note it down, Swami.' Swaminathan noted down on a paper, 'Vilord june-ear bat.' And looking up asked, 'How many?'

'Say three. Will that do, Mani?'

'Why waste money on three bats? Two will do. . . .'

'But suppose one breaks in the middle of a match?' Rajam asked.

'Do you suppose we are going to supply bats to our opponents? They will have to come provided with bats. We must make it clear.'

'Even then, if our bat breaks we may have to stop playing.'

'Two will do, Rajam, unless you want to waste money.'

Rajam's enthusiasm was great. He left his chair and sat on the arm of Mani's chair, gloating over the pictures of cricket goods in the catalogue. Swaminathan, though he was considered to be bit of a heretic, caught the enthusiasm and perched on the other arm of the chair. All the three devoured with their eyes the glossy pictures of cricket balls, bats, and nets.

In about an hour they selected from the catalogue their team's requirements. And then came the most difficult part of the whole affair—a letter to Messrs Binns, ordering goods. Bare courtesy made Rajam offer the authorship of the letter to Mani, who declined it. Swaminathan was forced to accept it in spite of his protests, and he sat for a long time chewing his pencil without producing a word: he had infinite trouble with spelling, and the more he tried to be correct the more muddled he was becoming; in the end he sat so long thinking of spelling that even such words as 'The' and 'And' became doubtful. Rajam took up the task himself. Half an hour later he placed on the table a letter:

'From
M.C.C. (And Victory Union Eleven),
Malgudi.

'To
Messrs Binns,
Sportsmen,
Mount Road,
Madras.

'Dear Sir,

'Please send to our team two junior willard bats, six balls, wickets and other things quick. It is very urgent. We shall send you money afterwards. Don't fear. Please be urgent.

'Yours obediently,

'CAPTAIN RAJAM (Captain).'

This letter received Swaminathan's benedictions. But Mani expressed certain doubts. He wanted to know whether 'Dear' could stand at the beginning of a letter to a perfect stranger. 'How can you call Binns "Dear Sir"? You must say "Sir".'

Rajam's explanation was: 'I won't say "Sir". It is said only by clerks. I am not Binns's clerk. I don't care to address him as "Sir".' So this letter went as it was.

After this exacting work they were resting, with a feeling of relief, when the postman came in with a card for Rajam. Rajam read it and cried, 'Guess who has written this?'

'Binns.'

'Silly. It must be our Head Master.'

'Somebody.'

'J. B. Hobbs.'

'It is from Sankar,' Rajam announced joyfully. 'Sankar! We had almost forgotten that old thief.' Swaminathan and Mani tore the card from Rajam's hand and read:

'MY DEAR FRIEND,

'I am studying here because my father came here. My mother is also here. All of us are here. And we will be only here. I am doing well. I hope you are doing well. It is very hot here. I had fever for three days and drank medicine. I hope I will read well and pass the examination. Is Swami and Mani doing well! It is very hot here. I am playing cricket now. I can't write more.

'With regards,

'your dearest friend,

'SANKAR.'

'P.S. Don't forget me.

'S.'

They were profoundly moved by this letter, and decided to reply at once.

Three letters were ready in an hour. Mani copied Sankar's letter verbatim. Swaminathan and Rajam wrote nearly similar letters: they said they were doing well by the grace of God; they hoped that Sankar would pass and also that he was doing well; then they said a lot about their cricket team and hoped that Sankar would become a member; they also said that Sankar's team might challenge them to a match.

The letters were put into a stamped envelope, and the flap was pasted. It was only then that they felt the need of knowing Sankar's address. They searched all parts of Sankar's card. Not a word anywhere, not even the name of the town he was writing from. They tried to get this out of the postmark. But a dark curved smudge on the stamp cannot be very illuminating.

III

The M.C.C. and its organizers had solid proof that they were persons of count when a letter from Binns came addressed to the Captain, M.C.C, Malgudi. It was a joy, touching that beautiful envelope and turning it over in the hand. Binns were the first to recognize the M.C.C, and Rajam took a vow that he would buy every bit that his team needed from that great firm. There were three implications in this letter that filled Rajam and his friends with rapture: (1) that His Majesty's post office recognized their team was proved by the fact that the letter addressed to the captain was promptly delivered to him; (2) that they were really recognized by such a magnificent firm as Binns of Madras was proved by the fact that Binns cared to reply in a full letter and not on a card, and actually typed the letter! (3) Binns sent under another cover carrying four annas postage a huge catalogue. What a tribute!

The letter informed the captain that Messrs Binns thanked him for his letter and would be much obliged to him if he would kindly remit 25 per cent with the order and the balance could be paid against the V.P.P. of the Railway Receipt.

Three heads buzzed over the meaning of this letter. The trouble was that they could not understand whether Binns were going to send the goods or not. Mani promised to unravel the letter if somebody would tell him what 'Obliged' meant. When they turned the pages of a dictionary and offered him the meaning, he was none the wiser. He felt that it was a meaningless word in that

place. 'One thing is clear,' said Rajam, 'Binns thanks us for our letter. So I don't think this letter could mean a refusal to supply us goods.' Swaminathan agreed with him, 'That is right. If he did not wish to supply you with things, would he thank you? He would have abused you.' He scrutinized the letter again to make sure that there was no mistake about the thanks.

'Why has the fool used this word?' Mani asked, referring to 'Obliged' which he could not pronounce. 'It has no meaning. Is he trying to make fun of us?'

'He says something about 25%. I wish I knew what it was,' said Rajam.

Swaminathan could hardly contain himself, 'I say, Rajam, I am surprised that you cannot understand this letter; you got 60 % in the last examination.'

'Have you any sense in you? What has that to do with this. Even a B.A. cannot understand this letter.'

In the end they came to the conclusion that the letter was sent to them by mistake. As far as they could see, the M.C.C. had written nothing in their previous letter to warrant such expressions as 'Obliged', 'Remit', and '25%'. It could not be that the great firm of Binns were trying to make fun of them. Swaminathan pointed out 'To the Captain, M.C.C' at the beginning of the letter. But he was told that it was also a part of the mistake.

This letter was put in a cover with a covering letter and dispatched. The covering letter said:

'We are very sorry that you sent me somebody's letter. We are returning this somebody's letter. Please send our things immediately.'

IV

The M.C.C. were an optimistic lot. Though they were still unhonoured with a reply to their second letter, they expected their goods to arrive with every post. After ten days they thought they would start playing with whatever was available till they got the real bats, etc. The bottom of a dealwood case provided them with three good bats, and Rajam managed to get three used tennis balls from his father's club. The Pea was there, offering four real stumps that he believed he had somewhere in his house. A neat slip of ground adjoining Rajam's bungalow was to be the pitch. Everything was ready. Even if Binns took a month more to manufacture the goods specially for the M.C.C. (as they faintly thought probable), there need be no delay in starting practice. By the time the real bats and the balls arrived, they would be in form to play matches.

Rajam had chosen from his class a few who, he thought, deserved to become members of the M.C.C.

At five o'clock on the opening day, the M.C.C. had assembled, all except the Pea, for whom Rajam was waiting anxiously. He had promised to bring the real stumps. It was half an hour past time and yet he was not to be seen anywhere.

At last his puny figure was discovered in the distance. There was a catch in Rajam's heart when he saw him. He strained his eyes to find out if the Pea had the things about him. But since the latter was coming from the west, he was seen in the blaze of the evening sun. All the twelve assembled in the field shaded their eyes and looked. Some said that he was carrying a bundle, while some thought that he was swinging his hands freely.

When he arrived, Rajam asked, 'Why didn't you tell us that you hadn't the stumps?'

'I have still got them,' protested the Pea, 'I shall bring them tomorrow. I am sure my father knows where they are kept.'

'You kept us waiting till now. Why did you not come earlier and tell us that you could not find them?'

'I tell you, I have been spending hours looking for them everywhere. How could I come here and tell you and at the same time search?'

A cloud descended upon the gathering. For over twenty hours every one among them had been dreaming of swinging a bat and throwing a ball. And they could have realized the dream but for the Pea's wickedness. Everybody looked at him sourly. He was isolated. Rajam felt like crying when he saw the dealwood planks and the tennis balls lying useless on the ground. What a glorious evening they could have had if only the stumps had been brought!

Amidst all this gloom somebody cast a ray of light by suggesting that they might use the compound wall of Rajam's bungalow as a temporary wicket.

A portion of the wall was marked off with a piece of charcoal, and the captain arranged the field and opened the batting himself.

Swaminathan took up the bowling. He held a tennis ball in his hand, took a few paces, and threw it over. Rajam swung the bat but missed it. The ball hit the wall right under the charcoal mark. Rajam was bowled out with the very first ball! There was a great shout of joy. The players pressed round Swaminathan to shake him and pat him on the back, he was given on the very spot the title, 'Tate'.

ANNOTATIONS

Page 72

Six weeks later: Connects with events in Swaminathan's life in the preceding chapter when Swami quits the Albert Mission school of Malgudi in a huff as a sequel to his innocent involvement in a nationalist demonstration, and joins the Board school.

Page 73

the Pea: Samuel, the Pea, Swami's tiny classfellow, nicknamed for his size:

The fourth friend was Samuel known as the 'pea' on account of his size. There was nothing outstanding about him. He was just ordinary, no outstanding virtue of muscle or intellect. He was as bad in Arithmetic as Swaminathan was. The bond between them was laughter. They were able to see together the same absurdities and incongruities in things. The most trivial and unnoticeable thing to others would tickle them to death. (Swami and Friends 9)

Mohammed of Gazni: Sultan Mahmud (971–C.1030) of Ghazna in Central Asia. Lured by the wealth of the temple towns in India, Mahmud conquered the Punjab for a launching platform and attacked India seventeen times.

Aurangazeb: (1618–1707). The last of the great Mughal emperors of India, who was a fervent Muslim.

Page 74

the Somnathpur God: The famous shrine of Lord Somnath (Lord Shiva) in the town of Somnath in Saurashtra in Gujarat, attacked many times by Sultan Mahmud of Ghazna. The last of these invasions was in 1027.

New-Moon days... Annual Ceremonies: New Moon days are considered inauspicious by Hindus, and nothing important is undertaken on these days. Annual ceremonies are performed in memory of one's *manes* (ancestral spirits), when a couple of Brahmins are ritually feasted to satisfy them.
Board High School... mentality: The class consciousness of Rajam is evident here. He is the son of the Police Superintendent and has been attending expensive Public Schools (Bishop Waller's, for example). He displays the condescension which results from the divide between a Public School and a government/municipal school.
anti-political: Means 'anti-nationalist' here.
Hobbs, Bradman, and Duleep: Cricketing legends.
Sir John Berry Hobbs (1882–1963): British cricketer, born in Cambridge. He made 3636 runs, including 12 centuries, in test matches against Australia, and a record number of 197 centuries and 61,167 runs in first-class cricket.
Sir Donald George Bradman (b. 1908): Australian cricketer, played for Australia 1928–48, and was captain from 1936. He set up many batting records, including the highest score (452 not out). Kumar *Sri Duleepsinhji (1905–59):* Indian cricketing prince after whom the Duleep trophy is named. He played for Cambridge, Sussex and England. He was a brilliant batsman and fielder; a worthy successor to his famous uncle K. S. Ranjitsinhji.

Page 75
M.C.C: An acronym for Marylebone Cricket Club, whose headquarters are at Lord's Cricket Ground, North London. Founded in 1787 by a group of noblemen, it had the responsibility for the making of cricket laws until 1969. The name the boys choose is an ironic reflection of the British influence on the Indian intelligentsia.
Jumping Stars: The name, incidentally, of the football 'club' in Madras of which little Narayan was a 'member'. It was Narayan's youngest brother Laxman, now the celebrated cartoonist, who played cricket in Mysore, and Narayan even chided him for it on one occasion. However, in *Swami and Friends* Narayan brings in cricket, probably because cricket, rather than football, goes with the kind of snobbery affected by the boys in the story, in an unselfconscious absorption of the adult world around them.

Page 76
The Government may not recognize...name: What Swami is thinking of is the registration of the team's name as a trade mark.

Page 77
Rolls-Royce: The British motor car that was at one time the most expensive and the most prestigious—an imperialist status symbol, like the gun-salute.

Page 78
Vilord june-ear bat: Charming indigenization of the pronunciation. The same sensitivity and imagination give us not only Sankar's letter, but the writing styles of the other letters in the novel as well.

Page 80
It was a joy, touching that beautiful envelope...: Narayan was twenty-four when he wrote *Swami and Friends;* but the most remarkable aspect of Narayan's achievement in the first novel is that he enters the child's world on the child's terms—as he does later the world of youth in his second novel, *The Bachelor of Arts.* See later: 'For over twenty hours everyone among them had been dreaming of swinging a bat and throwing a ball.... What a glorious evening they could have had if only the stumps had been brought!' (p. 82).

Page 83
Tate: Maurice William Tate (1895–1956), the English bowler who advanced overnight to become the greatest fast medium bowler of his era. He is one of the three cricketers in history to have scored more than 1000 runs and to have taken 200 wickets in a first-class season. He performed this feat thrice, in three successive years from 1923 to 1925.

SUGGESTED READING

Narayan, R. K., *My Days,* New York: Viking, 1974.

———, *A Horse and Two Goats,* New York: Viking, 1970.

Ram, Susan, and N. Ram, *R. K. Narayan, The Early Years: 1906–45,* New Delhi: Penguin, 1996.

Walsh, William, *R. K. Narayan: A Critical Appreciation,* New Delhi: Allied, 1983.

VAIKOM MUHAMMAD BASHEER
(1908–94)

Vaikom Muhammad Basheer, the son of a timber merchant, was born in Vaikom in south Kerala. While at school, coming under the spell of Mahatma Gandhi who visited Vaikom in 1924, Basheer ran away to Calicut in Malabar, the hub of the National Movement. Subsequently he was imprisoned for participating in the Salt Satyagraha (1930). The tortures he suffered there prompted him to reject *ahimsa* or non-violence and when released from jail he joined *Ujjeevanam*, the organ of an extremist political group. With the banning of the paper and the seizure of anti-British literature, Basheer left Kerala, evading arrest. For nearly a decade he travelled all over India, reaching as far as Arabia. His incredibly strange experiences during his sojourn have found their way into his quasi-autobiographical fiction, mostly narrated through an 'I' persona. Returning to Kerala after his peregrinations Basheer went to jail for a second time. 'Mathiluka' (Walls), 'Tiger', and several other stories are fictional depictions of his prison experiences. Many of the characters we find in 'The Card-Sharper's Daughter' are drawn on jail birds with whom he had struck up an acquaintance. After being released, Basheer worked for a paper in Madras and finally, returning to Kerala, started the Circle Book House in Ernakulam. This had to be wound up later when Basheer underwent long treatment for an attack of insanity which erupted now and then in later years.

Basheer earned fame as a writer with his first novella, *Balyakalasakhi* (Childhood Friend, 1944). This, and his other two novellas, *Patbumma's Goat* (1959) and 'Me grandad 'ad an elephant!' (1961), when translated into English, brought him international renown. The only play he wrote was *Kathabeejam* (The Seed of the Story) drawing on his own experiences as a struggling writer. The sombre tone of *Sabdangal* (Voices) and some of his poetic prose pieces such as 'Anarghanimisham' (The Invaluable Moment) and 'Sandhyapranamam' (An Evening Prayer), depicting man's existential anguish, show a facet of Basheer which is not evident in the rest of his corpus. Basheer grew up in a milieu lacking in the cultural stimulants that generally nurture the creative impulse. 'Agonizing experiences and a pen' were his only equipment when circumstances propelled him to write. Hence it was by forging his own style that Basheer became the master of colloquial speech and racy humour. This singles him out from his distinguished contemporaries like Karoor Neelakanta Pillai (1898–1975), Thakazhi Sivasankara Pillai (1912–99), S. K. Pottekkat (1913–82) and Lalitambika Antharjanam (1909–87) with whom he shared only a certain social conjuncture and consciousness, and not the literary conventions of Sanskritized Malayalam.

The theme of 'The Card-Sharper's Daughter' is the debunking of Pokker by the slow-witted Muthapa. Their rivalries are raised to mock-epic heights with Basheer's characteristic irony. The trivia of a domestic conflict are given a political dimension to make a travesty of the political feuds and slogan-shouting so common in Kerala. For Basheer the realist, the unprepossessing, cross-eyed Muthapa's love for Zainaba is as amenable to romantic treatment as the lofty passion of any chevalier for his *grande dame.* Basheer's native talent as a raconteur of tales is evident here. Published in the original as *Mucheettukalikkarante Makal,* K. M. Sherrif's is the first English translation of this story. Basheer made minor alterations to the text several times, and Sherrif has taken into account the various published versions of the story. This translation has managed to capture as best it can the atmosphere and raw humour of the original, whose punch derives from the lively use of the Mappila dialect of the Malayalee Muslims interspersed with Arabic words, the crisp language of card-sharping, the good-humoured satire of crooks and of the corrupt police, and the rhetoric of left slogans.

THE CARD-SHARPER'S DAUGHTER

The moral of this story may as well be delivered right at the beginning. Girls will find it neither amusing nor enlightening. Anyway, here it is. If you happen to have daughters, steel your heart and murder them all in cold blood!

Now don't think that these are my views. I earnestly hope and pray that none of the many honourable ladies among my readers, incensed by this blatantly misogynist observation, condemns me to eternal damnation. They should target Ottakkannan Pokker instead!

Ottakkannan Pokker is the tragic protagonist of this story. Mandan Muthapa may be loosely described as the villain, though, as the story progresses, he steadily rises in stature to become the hero, the chivalrous knight who takes up arms against Pokker. Zainaba is Muthapa's comrade-in-arms in the battle.

The constables of the village outpost, both stooges of the tyrannical regime, and Thorappan Avaran and Driver Pappunni, the two master rogues, were out of station. Anavari Raman Nair and Ponkurissu Thoma, bigwigs of the local criminal fraternity, were holding the fort for them. Ettukali Mammoonhu, their protege, was always at hand. So were the other villagers, who were more than twenty-two hundred in number. All of them were peace-lovers, they had nothing to do with warmongering reactionaries.

These are the essential facts which I, as a humble chronicler, would like my readers to acquaint themselves with. Apart from these, it would be prudent to note the presence of a floating population of about twenty-six hundred men and women who appeared only on Tuesdays and Saturdays, the village market-days. Their role was confined to buying and selling and making a great ruckus—with a few scuffles thrown in. Ottakkannan Pokker and Mandan Muthapa were artists who rubbed shoulders with this multitude as they pursued their respective vocations. Zainaba also belonged to the ranks of the people, though she was seldom seen in their midst. Her creative endeavours were shrouded in mystery.

Would you ever trust your daughters if you knew what they were up to? Why do they cause the best-laid schemes of their fathers to go awry? What do daughters know of the agonies of a father's heart!

I must confess that, after interviewing the major characters of the story, I felt a certain partiality towards some of them and consequently lent them my moral support. I record here the whole story for the benefit of students of history.

I shall begin with Ottakkannan Pokker. As the sobriquet prefixed to his name indicates, he had only one eye. It had been damaged beyond repair in one of the heroic adventures of his salad days. It was true that certain intellectuals in the locality surreptitiously referred to him as 'that one-eyed monkey.' But never mind that. When this story begins, he was forty-nine years old. His complexion could be described as fair. The real colour of his teeth was a well-concealed secret. The visible colour was a dull red, owing to the fact that Pokker was a voracious betel-chewer. And by virtue of his profession, 'Ottakkannan Pokker, the card-sharper' was how he was popularly referred to.

I suppose you have deduced from what has already been said that Zainaba was Pokker's daughter. Nineteen years of age, she was the village beauty. She had to be married off to some hard-working young man. This was what drove Ottakkannan Pokker to work tirelessly, day in and day out.

Pokker had already accumulated a sum of one hundred and twenty rupees towards this end. Now, what happened to this money? Zainaba didn't steal it. Anavari, Ponkurissu, Thorappan, Ettukali and their admirers were all innocent of the crime though, as a rule, the institution of private property was anathema to them. The two constables had nothing to do with it either. Mandan Muthapa? Certainly not! The fact is, nobody stole it. What happened to it then? Wait, I am coming to that.

The focus of the narrative now shifts to Mandan Muthapa, a young man of twenty-one, jet-black in complexion and slightly cross-eyed. However, he always had a charming smile on his face. Like Zainaba, he had lost his mother in his childhood. His father had died a martyr's death in prison after a pitched battle with a bunch of beastly policemen over some misunderstanding about a burglary. As far as he could remember, he did not have any kith or kin. People just called him 'Mandan Muthapa, the pickpocket.'

'Mandan' or 'nitwit' had been prefixed to Muthapa's name by none other than Pokker. In a way, Pokker was Muthapa's mentor, having taught him the technique of exhaling smoke through one's nose. Though Muthapa was required to pay a fee of one rupee for the lesson, he had unbelted only five-and-a-half annas. The loss still rankled. 'That bastard Mandan owes me ten-and-a-half annas,' Pokker would wrathfully say, 'I taught him to blow smoke through his nose.' This claim dealt a crushing blow to Muthapa's ambitions. Muthapa had just begun his career as an apprentice to Anavari Raman Nair and Ponkurissu Thoma. Pokker's statement prompted these gentlemen to have second thoughts about their young apprentice, and Muthapa was left to fend for himself in a wicked world. Who would employ a Mandan—a dunce—when bright young boys jostled for attention?

Before he started picking pockets, Mandan Muthapa had tried to enroll himself as Pokker's pupil in card-sharping. He had managed to get his case recommended by a few influential well-wishers as well. But Pokker had refused to oblige. 'Get lost, you donkey. It needs boys with brains to do this stuff.'

Pokker was right there. Brains were an asset in any profession and card-sharping demanded an exceptionally high level of intelligence—and, of course, capital. Pokker had both. His kit consisted of a pack of cards, an old issue of *Malayala Manorama* and a handful of small stones. The stones served as paperweights when the musty newspaper was spread out and the pack of cards placed on it. Shuffling the cards briskly, Pokker would take out three from the pack, one joker and two numbered cards. The next step was to exhibit these cards face-up for his clients to take a good look at them, the joker in one hand and the numbered cards in the other. But some vigorous sales-talk was necessary before the clients could be won over completely. So Pokker would clear his throat and unleash his oratorical skills on them. 'Hai raja... come on everybody... double your money, folks... two for one, four for two, the joker makes your fortune. Never mind if you place your money on the numbered cards. It's your alms for a poor man... hai raja...'

Pokker would flick the cards facedown on the paper with a whirring motion. It was the gamblers' responsibility to observe the movement of the cards carefully. Hawk-eyed, they would stare before placing their bets on the cards of their choice. Most of them placed anna coins and one-rupee notes on the cards, though there were also some who wagered as much as five or ten rupees. But when the cards were turned, they would find that the joker had eluded them—as always. Thus, each round ended with defeat for the valiant people and success for the wily Pokker. He would calmly scoop up the money, of which two rupees went to the local constabulary.

But it was not amusing to play to lose all the time. So Pokker hit upon a brilliant strategy. On an average, the people won nearly six times out of ten. Amazing! But, there was a catch. For 'people,' read 'friends and apprentices of Pokker whose identities were unknown to the market crowd.' There was no fraud in this really!

Yet what a world of difference there was between Ottakkannan Pokker's and Mandan Muthapa's professions! Contrary to popular opinion, there is nothing demeaning about a pickpocket's work. It has made amazing strides in many countries of the world. There are even colleges to train aspiring pickpockets. That apart, it is a profession which requires unwavering concentration, infinite patience, an eye for detail and unshaken faith in the adage 'silence is golden.' And, as I have already mentioned, some brains would certainly help. Did Mandan Muthapa have any brains? Well... grit and determination will see the professional pickpocket through many a crisis.

As for capital, long nimble fingers and a shawl are the only tools required. Like all committed artists, a pickpocket has to have a finger on the pulse of the people. Not for him the solitary existence of the ivory tower. In other words, a pickpocket is essentially a social being, sharing the joys and sorrows of the people. 'Community living' is the pickpocket's motto. Weddings, funerals, cattle-trading posts, carnivals, processions, wrestling matches, political meetings—wherever human beings congregate—he presents himself to unburden the unwary of their filthy lucre.

The modus operandi is simple. Single out a man from the crowd who looks well-to-do, cover his pocket with the shawl and, with a quick movement of the long fingers, deftly remove the wallet or pouch. Speed is of the essence and it can be achieved only through sustained practice. But that is not all. The loot has to be passed on to an apprentice who immediately effects a vanishing trick.

Unfortunately, of all the requirements listed above, a shawl and long nimble fingers were all that Muthapa possessed. His height of six feet and two inches was a liability. He was a full head taller than most men in the crowd that thronged the village on market-days. No sooner did he appear on the scene than there would be a cry from the crowd, 'Hey you, be careful! Mandan Muthapa has taken a liking to you.' A typical instance of the scant respect society gives to artists!

However, none of these zealots belonged to the village. They were all outsiders, henchmen of the hated establishment. They had closed their ranks against Mandan Muthapa. Unlike the workers of certain political parties, Muthapa did not let out hoarse-throated slogans, condemning his detractors for being 'bourgeois reactionaries.' He merely flashed his charming, innocent smile that mesmerized them and unsuspecting bystanders alike. But not the village constables. They squeezed Muthapa to the tune of one rupee each market-day. The politically-conscious villagers had no use for these representatives of the powers that be and opposed this highhandedness. But that made no difference to the constables who were determined to have their cut of Muthapa's earnings. How could Muthapa manage when, in spite of his toils, he earned next to nothing on several days? To make matters worse, Ottakkannan Pokker was always at hand to give prosecution evidence against Muthapa. 'That bastard Mandan cleaned up ten rupees today. I saw the racket with my own eyes.'

'You one-eyed devil!' Mandan Muthapa would mutter, 'I'll gouge out your good eye one of these days.'

The equation was now clear and known to one and all. The arch-enemies had taken to the battlefield. Mandan Muthapa, the pickpocket, universally acknowledged to be a nitwit, and Ottakkannan Pokker, the card-sharper, whose wits never deserted him. The tale which I am about to unfold before you describes how Mandan Muthapa, the nitwit, vanquished his nimble-witted adversary and won the hand of...well, I should not kill the suspense. Let me begin at the beginning.

It was a Saturday. Ottakkannan Pokker had presented himself under the ancient silk-cotton tree in the marketplace well before the clamour of the market-day had begun. Mandan Muthapa, having had no breakfast, was feeling rather down in the dumps that morning. There were no good Samaritans around to buy him even a cup of tea. But as he came down the lane, hungry and dejected, there appeared before him a man in a long jubba. This man wore a gold-plated wristwatch and had an expensive looking fountain pen clipped to the pocket of his jubba. Muthapa's heart skipped a beat. As the man walked on jauntily with the air of a millionaire, oblivious of his surroundings, puffing at a cigarette, Muthapa relieved him of his wallet.

It was one of the most successful jobs Muthapa had pulled off. But the contents of the wallet did not delight him. Five-and-a-half annas and the photograph of a film actress who wore a nose-stud were all that he got for his pains. 'Damn her nose-stud!' Muthapa cursed, tearing the photograph into bits. 'Him and his almighty airs! The miser!'

The newly-opened restaurant was doing brisk business. Muthapa decided to give it a try. He seated himself next to a fat man whose side-pocket looked promising. But nothing came of it. Muthapa quietly finished the snacks and tea the waiter had served him unsolicited. It came to four annas. He bought beedis for half-an-anna, and with the remaining capital of one anna, presented himself before Ottakkannan Pokker.

'Hai raja...come on...two for one...any mandan ass can try...' Ottakkannan Pokker said, before throwing the cards facedown on a sheet of paper. Muthapa placed the anna on what he judged to be the joker. 'Get lost, you ass,' Pokker told him gently as he turned the card. It was a numbered card.

'Would you like another try?' Pokker asked with a mocking wink.

Muthapa had run out of money. Lighting a beedi, he walked away from the crowd, towards the solitude of the river. How sad is the plight of a poor artist! How agonizing it is to think of what might have been! In his heart, Mandan Muthapa worshipped Thorappan Avaran, Driver Pappunni, Ponkurissu Thoma and Anavari Raman Nair as his mentors. If only they would accept him as their pupil. That Ottakkannan Pokker, curse him! He had spoilt everything.

Lost in thought, Muthapa walked on. His steps took him down the path by the river. The market landing was crowded with boats. There were large mounds of tapioca, coconuts, bananas and a variety of vegetables all around. As he gazed listlessly at the boats loaded with merchandise, Muthapa witnessed a miracle!

A bunch of bananas dragged itself out of a mound, climbed over the side of the boat and leaped into the river! It was not one of those accidents when things topple into the river from overloaded boats. The bunch of bananas did it slowly, deliberately—as if it were alive!

This set Muthapa thinking. Were the bananas possessed by a

devil? he wondered. Consigned to the plant kingdom by nature, they would certainly require a devil's services to 'walk away' as they had. They were now moving steadily in the water towards the next landing where Ottakkannan Pokker lived. A row of silk-cotton trees, that stretched between the two landings, functioned as a wide curtain.

His curiosity aroused, Muthapa walked towards the landing downstream, following the bananas with his eyes. Suddenly, startling him, appeared Zainaba, Pokker's only daughter. Crouching in the shadow of the trees, she was pulling at a strong string that stretched towards the river. Soon she pulled up the bunch of bananas which had reached its destination. There was a fishing hook attached to the bunch, Muthapa noted.

In a flash, everything fell into place, like the pieces of a jigsaw puzzle. It was a simple process. Swim down to the market landing under cover of the bushes with a hook attached to a long line. Fix the hook to a bunch of bananas and swim back downstream, unwinding the line gently. Hide behind the clump of silk-cotton trees, pull the bananas, and they are yours.

Mandan Muthapa was distressed. There was nothing wrong in men stealing or picking pockets. But for a woman to do so... He stood transfixed, afflicted by Zainaba's indiscretion.

Zainaba climbed ashore with the bunch of bananas, water dripping from her wet clothes, She had no inkling of Muthapa's presence. When her eyes fell on him, she dropped the bananas with a gasp. Her face turned a deep purple, and then white as chalk.

'Zainaba!' There was love and anguish in Muthapa's voice.

'O!' Zainaba answered in a broken voice.

'Do you think what you have done is right?'

'Nnnno...'

'Will you do it again?' 'No.'

'Change your clothes and wipe yourself dry. You will catch a cold.'

Zainaba ran, without taking the bananas. Muthapa carried them home for her. She had a small restaurant there. Besides tea, it served puttu, boiled black gram, appam, vada and bananas. She gave credit to some of her regular customers, among whom were Anavari Raman Nair, Ponkurissu Thoma and Ettukali Mammoonhu. When they reached her house, she invited Muthapa in for tea with idiyappam and bananas.

Muthapa testifies to all these facts. Zainaba, however, refused to reply when she was confronted by this chronicler and asked whether she loved Muthapa. But she was quite certain that Muthapa was not a mandan. 'Bapa says that out of spite,' she said.

Ottakkannan Pokker was completely ignorant of all this. He was not suspicious of Zainaba. Preoccupied with the task of putting by some money for her wedding, he did not notice such things. An honest and hard-working boy had to be found. She should have a few pairs of earrings and necklaces for the wedding. These were his concerns.

That day, Pokker was returning home with a bag of provisions he had bought at the market. The first sight that greeted his eyes when he stepped into the house was that of Mandan Muthapa, his head reclining in Zainaba's lap.

What more was required to break a poor father's heart? A dark, cross-eyed, stupid pickpocket nestling in your daughter's lap! One rarely comes across a father who would find it funny.

'Bapa!' Zainaba leapt up in terror as she pushed Muthapa away.

But Mandan Muthapa merely flashed his charming smile.

Ottakkannan Pokker was furious. He flung a piece of tapioca at Muthapa which struck him square on his chest. Though it hurt him considerably, Muthapa, without removing the smile from his face, picked it up, peeled it gently and nibbled at it. 'Mama, you know I am going to marry Zainaba,' he said.

Now this was a double-edged statement. Firstly, 'mama' is a term used to address one's maternal uncle or wife's father. As we know, neither of these relationships existed between Ottakkannan Pokker and Mandan Muthapa. Was Muthapa taking a leap into the future? Besides, as you might have noticed, Muthapa's statement was a bold assertion, not a humble request like 'May I beg for the hand of your fair daughter' etcetera.

Ottakkannan Pokker shook with rage. 'Get out of my house, you thieving scoundrel!' he screamed.

'Mama, forgive me for all I have said and done to you. Zainaba says I should stop picking pockets. So I'm not going to any more.'

'I see. You are taking to begging instead.'

'I want to set up a small restaurant,' Muthapa continued, ignoring the sarcasm. 'Mama, will you lend me ten rupees for it?'

'What about the ten-and-a-half annas you owe me for teaching you to smoke through the nose?'

Mandan Muthapa ignored that too. 'Any day before the end of the month would suit me for the wedding.'

'Get out, you blasted Jew!' Ottakkannan Pokker roared. 'Don't get any such ideas as long as I am alive.'

But the veiled threat did not deter Muthapa. 'Mama, I'll marry Zainaba long before you die.'

'Get out!'

Mandan Muthapa walked away calmly.

This was the beginning of a long struggle, a fight to the finish. The news spread like wildfire. The villagers were merely amused at first. But soon they split into opposing camps. In the beginning, the two constables were staunch supporters of Ottakkannan Pokker. But soon they, along with the vast majority of the villagers, shifted their loyalties to Mandan Muthapa. There was a good reason for such a move. But more about it later.

Where did Zainaba's loyalties lie? the villagers wondered.

'Zainaba's with me,' declared Mandan Muthapa, drawing himself to his full height and thumping his chest.

'She's my daughter,' Ottakkannan Pokker said with some amount of confidence.

But the fact was that nobody really knew anything about Zainaba's loyalties. Meanwhile, Anavari Raman Nair and Ponkurissu Thoma made a joint statement, 'It is a battle for Zainaba's heart.'

To the villagers, this sounded like one of the most stupid things they had ever heard. Did the duo really believe that the union of two hearts was all that mattered? There was an obstinate father to be reckoned with. That and the hundred and twenty rupees, his life's earnings. Ottakkannan Pokker was in a position to marry Zainaba to any young man of his choice. This was the state of affairs when Muthapa declared war.

Right from the beginning, Mandan Muthapa's offensive met with remarkable success. He was the universally acclaimed leader of the masses.

Pokker was denounced as a hoarder, a black-marketeer, and

above all, a bourgeois reactionary. 'Mandan Muthapa zindabad!'

'Ottakkannan Pokker murdabad!'

Slogans rent the air. There was no dearth of people to buy tea and lunch for Muthapa whenever he needed them. On the other hand, Pokker found it difficult to get even a pinch of slaked lime for his betel-and-nut.

It was a Tuesday. The marketplace was beginning to bustle with buyers and sellers. Mandan Muthapa appeared without his customary shawl. He held a one-rupee note in his hand. He had pinched it with his teeth. 'This is a lucky note,' he was heard telling a man in the crowd, 'Zainaba gave it to me.'

Muthapa headed straight for Ottakkannan Pokker's gambling corner. As usual, a small crowd had collected in front of it.

'Hai raja, come on. Double your money. The joker is your lucky boy. Keep your eyes peeled. Hai raja...'

Mandan Muthapa clutched the one-rupee note between his thumb and forefinger and sniffed at it rather noisily. Ottakkannan Pokker looked up at Muthapa and continued with his sales-talk, inserting a couple of unusual expressions in between. 'Hai raja, double your money. Any sucker can try his luck, any stuffed monkey can try his luck. The joker is your lucky boy...'

Pokker flicked the cards facedown on the paper. Mandan Muthapa scrutinized the cards carefully and placed his one-rupee note on one of them. Pokker winced as if he had been pricked with a pin. In twenty-two years of card-sharping, nobody had placed his money on the joker without Pokker's express permission. Perhaps a handful of lucky chaps had got the card right purely by accident. Their number was, however, too small for Pokker to remember. There was absolutely no connection between card-sharping and luck. The golden rule was that Pokker should always win and the market-day crowd lose.

Ottakkannan Pokker turned the cards. There was a gasp from the crowd. Muthapa's one-rupee note had been on the joker. And Pokker grudgingly gave him another rupee.

'Hai raja, two for one, four for two... open to all and sundry...' The game resumed.

As before, Mandan Muthapa looked carefully at each card before placing his two rupees on one of them. Ottakkannan Pokker turned the cards. The joker again for Muthapa! He now had four rupees.

When Muthapa's luck persisted in the next round, Pokker lost his temper. The crowd let out a whoop of joy.

Muthapa's luck held out. He gazed at the windfall in his hand—sixteen rupees—and rustled the notes gently. He took out the one-rupee note, which had been his capital when he started, kissed it reverentially and tied it at the end of his mundu. He then announced his future plans to the crowd, 'I am through with picking pockets. I am going to set up a tea shop.'

Mandan Muthapa walked away triumphantly, accompanied by his fellow artists—Anavari Raman Nair, Ponkurissu Thoma and Ettukali Mammoonhu. Behind them came a host of villagers, their spirit for battle aroused. Soon the whole village learned of Muthapa's triumph. There was universal rejoicing. It was a victory for the people!

There was not a soul to commiserate with the vanquished Pokker. But then, one can't expect people to sympathize with black-marketeers and lackeys of reactionary regimes.

'Daughter, I lost fifteen rupees today,' Pokker told Zainaba mournfully that night. 'That scoundrel did me in.'

She said nothing. There was neither sympathy nor exhilaration in her expression. But Pokker's grief knew no bounds. 'I am not finished,' he said, regaining his composure, 'Let that Mandan have another try. I'll skin him. Pokker doesn't take things lying down.'

Come market-day, the hawkers arrived with their wares. Men and women jostled as they sought to make their bargains. Muthapa's tea shop had opened just a few days before. As a matter of fact, no tea was served there. Only coffee with jaggery, and boiled gram to go with it. It was an apology for a tea shop, functioning in the open space between two buildings, sheets of cloth hung up on poles to make an enclosure. An old bench, the only item of furniture, and two glasses to serve coffee in. Noisily stirring the jaggery in a glass with a spoon, he invited his customers, 'Hai, Mandan's coffee! Sizzling hot! Have a sip folks, gives you more than your money's worth.'

The coffee and the boiled black gram were sold out before noon.

Muthapa counted his earnings and wrapped the notes and coins in a piece of paper. With this packet, he presented himself before Pokker.

Ottakkannan Pokker lost twenty rupees that day. When he told Zainaba about it that night, she merely shrugged her shoulders. 'Oh, I suppose everybody has caught on to the trick by now.'

'Caught on! Listen, you stupid... Nobody caught on to it in the last twenty-two years. You mean to say that bastard Mandan did it in a couple of days?'

Zainaba said nothing.

'I taught that stingy Jew how to blow out smoke through his nose!'

A dozen market-days passed by. Mandan Muthapa continued to subject Ottakkannan Pokker to humiliating defeats. Pokker was now at the end of his tether, broke and neck-deep in debt. And finally, he admitted defeat. 'Son, leave me alone, please,' he pleaded with Muthapa. Til give you five rupees on each market-day.'

'I don't want your money,' said the long-suffering Muthapa. 'I have my shop now. Let me marry Zainaba, and I'll quit card-sharping for good.'

Marriage to Zainaba—Muthapa was firm on this compromise formula. So were the valiant villagers.

Ottakkannan Pokker ran from pillar to post for help. He beseeched the two constables to come to his aid. He unburdened his heart to Anavan Raman Nair, Ponkurissu Thoma and Ettukali Mammoonhu. But his pleas fell on deaf ears. 'Get Zainaba married to that fellow, man,' they told him in one voice.

'But, my dear sir, he is a mandan.'

'There you go again!'

Pokker was left with no option.

The whole village attended the wedding. Muthapa treated them to betel-nut, beedis and sherbet. At night, there was a display of fireworks sponsored by the villagers.

It was a happy ending to a long conflict. But not quite. Ottakkannan Pokker was heartbroken. He quit card-sharping. He lost his appetite and always wore a melancholy expression on his face. He hated everyone—Zainaba, Anavari Raman Nair, Ponkurissu

Thoma, the constables, Ettukali Mammoonhu, and the decadent social order which sustained them. Pokker stopped eating altogether, determined to fast unto death.

The kindhearted villagers intervened. After a lot of cajoling, they succeeded in persuading Pokker to live with Zainaba and Muthapa in the annexe to their hotel. Yes, the make-shift tea shop had graduated into a proper hotel! Zainaba's puttu and boiled black gram were in great demand.

The enterprise was wholeheartedly supported by Zainaba's regular customers—Anavari Raman Nair, Ponkurissu Thoma, their protege Ettukali Mammoonhu, and the two constables. Like them, Pokker could eat his fill and he was required to do no work.

But there was something which tormented Pokker like a thorn in his flesh. How could Mandan Muthapa place his money unfailingly on the joker all the time? Unable to bear it any longer, he put the question to Muthapa himself.

'Just brains,' Muthapa replied, tapping his forehead.

Pokker knew it was too good to be true. Where could Mandan Muthapa get brains from, he who was willing to *part* with precious money for learning to let out smoke through the nose?

When Pokker persisted, Muthapa revealed the secret. 'It was my wife's brain wave.'

Zainaba's brain wave! Mandan Muthapa produced the evidence. The corners of all the jokers in the pack had been marked out by small holes made with a safety pin!

'What do you think, son?' Ottakkannan Pokker asked me, 'Can you ever trust your daughters?'

Well, what can one say...!

Translated from the Malayalam
by K. M. Sherrif

ANNOTATIONS

Page 88
Ottakkannan: One-eyed.
Pokker: A corruption of Bakar, as in 'Aboo Bakar'.
Mandan: Slow-witted.

Muthapa: A corruption of the name Mustafa.
village: In the original, 'sthalam'. It means 'place', and is described thus in *Sthalathe Pradhana Divyan* (The Chief Godman of the Place): 'The inhabitants of the sthalam claim that they were the first to discover the Sun God. Similarly, they say that they invented the shaving razor… fire… card-sharping… cock fighting, the bullock cart [etc]. According to Muzhayan [full of bumps] Nanu, the sthalam is at the dead centre of the earth and Kaduvakkuzhi Hill is at the centre of the sthalam. Its circumference is nine miles. The wide world beyond its periphery is the alien region of reactionaries.'
stooges: In the original, the constables are referred to as 'moorachi', meaning reactionary.
tyrannical regime: An allusion to the Establishment and its law and order system as perceived by a radical. *Thorappan:* Mole.
Anavari: Mistaking an elephant for a dung heap, Raman Nair attempted to collect it stealthily, thereby incurring the nickname 'anavari' (elephant-grabber).
Ettukali: Spider. Mammoonhu was so called because of his small head and long, drooping moustache. Such sobriquets are common in Kerala. All the characters mentioned feature in several stories of Basheer. Detailed accounts of their exploits can be found in 'Anavariyum Ponkurissum' (The Elephant Grabber and the Golden Cross), 'Sthalathe Pradhana Divyan' (The Chief Godman of the Place), and 'Oru Bhagavad Gitayum Kure Mulakalum' (One Bhagavad Gita and Several Breasts).
Mammoonhu: A corruption of Mohammed Kunju.
Ponkurissu: A cross made of gold. Thoma had once stolen a gold cross from a church.

Page 90
Malayala Manorama: The name of a popular newspaper in Malayalam.

Page 92
Tow *one-eyed devil…days':* In the original, 'You one-eyed Iblees [the Devil], one-eyed monkey, you will lose your other eye too'.

Page 94
puttu: A preparation made with steamed rice flour and grated co-

conut.

Page 96
Jew: Used here as a term of abuse. Like Pokker, Muthapa was a Muslim.

Page 97
lime for his betel-and-nut: Here, some sentences in the original have been omitted in translation. They may be translated thus:
'To Pokker's anguished query "What wrong have I done?", the people in one voice answered: "Aren't you the capitalist reactionary hoarding that girl and abetting the powers that be to sell her in the black market?"'
"Come what may", said Pokker, "I shall not give Zainaba's hand in marriage to that moron."
In a way it was a popular movement, Mandan Muthapa only lending it his leadership. Expressing their solidarity with him were worthies like Anavari Raman Nair, Ponkurissu Thoma, and Ettukali Mammoonhu. The entire populace of the sthalam took part in the movement.'

Page 98
mundu: An apparel like the dhoti.
Mandan's coffee: 'Wayanadan coffee' in the original. Coffee is grown in Wayanad in northern Kerala.

SUGGESTED READING

Basheer, Vaikom Muhammad, 'Me grandad 'ad an elephant!': *Three Stories of Muslim Life in South India,* trans. R. E. Asher et al., Edinburgh: University of Edinburgh Press, 1980 and New Delhi: Penguin India, 1992.

————, *The Magic Cat,* trans. N. Kunju, Trissur: Kerala Sahitya Akademi, 1978.

Ravindran, Vanajam ed., *Vaikom Muhammad Basheer: Short Stories,* New Delhi: Katha/Rupa, 1996.

SAADAT HASAN MANTO
(1912–55)

Saadat Hasan Manto was born in Samrala, a small town in Punjab, in a Kashmiri family. He received his early education in Amritsar and then joined Aligarh Muslim University. Manto could not cope with the restrictive academic environment there and left the University without completing his graduation. Subsequently, he discovered that he was suffering from tuberculosis and was advised complete rest in the hills for three months in 1935. Manto went to Bombay in 1937 and worked as editor first of *Mussavar* (an Urdu magazine) and then of *Caravan.* He returned to Delhi in 1941 where he worked for a while with All India Radio and wrote over a hundred radio plays in less than two years. Some of his most powerful stories such as 'Hatak' (Insult) and 'Bu' (Odour) were written during this period. From 1943 onwards Manto was associated with the Bombay film industry and wrote extensively for films. This was the phase in his life when he obtained prosperity and fame. The Partition of the Subcontinent in 1947 tragically altered the course of Manto's life. Although emotionally he could not accept the reality of the division of the country, Manto migrated to Lahore in 1948. He failed to get a regular job there and lived in great poverty. However, despite ill health and financial constraints, Manto's creative energy was undiminished and he spent the remaining years of his life writing parables of lost reason, demonic horror, and unimaginable violence, such as 'Toba Tek Singh', '1919 Ki Ek Baat' (Something About 1919), 'Mozel', 'Titwal Ka Kutta' (The Dog of Titwal), 'Khol Do' (Open It), and the very short stories, some of which are barely a paragraph each, collected in *Siyah Hasbeye* (Black Margins). Towards the end of his life Manto went into a deep depression and sought refuge in a mental asylum to cure himself of alcoholism. He died in 1955, without being able to locate his lost homeland, like his protagonist Toba Tek Singh.

Manto played a formative role in the development of the Urdu short story, along with Rajinder Singh Bedi and Krishan Chander, who had begun to write in the nineteen thirties. Premchand had earlier brought Urdu fiction out of the unreal realms of fantasy and romance. Manto and his contemporaries such as Ismat Chughtai and Ahmad Nadim Qasmi further developed this trend towards realistic representation, exploring the truth of human existence with keen psychological insight and down-to-earth realism. Manto began his writing career with the translation of Victor Hugo's novel, *The Last Days of the Condemned,* and Oscar Wilde's play, *Vera.* He read Russian and French literature extensively and was deeply influenced by the stories of Guy de Maupassant. Like Maupassant, he paid careful attention to the structure of the story, especially to the ending, using each detail with economy and brevity. Manto's stories focus on the marginalized in society-prostitutes, pimps, criminals, deviants. The stark truthfulness and the sardonic humour with which they are portrayed unmask the hypocrisy and cant of middle class pretensions. In Manto's words, 'the wrong which is ascribed to my stories is in fact the rot of the system'. In fact, Manto had to defend himself in court against charges of obscenity on account of five of his stories: 'Kali Salwar' (The Black Salwar), 'Dhuan' (Smoke), 'Bu' (Odour), 'Khol Do' (Open It), and 'Thanda Gosht' (Cold Flesh). Manto was deeply embroiled in controversies throughout his life. There are countless anecdotes about his eccentricities, his impatient temperament, and his iconoclastic ideas.

'Toba Tek Singh' was published in 1953 in an Urdu magazine, *Savera.* Like many of Manto's stories written between 1948 and 1955, it renders the pain and trauma of the experiences of the Partition with acute sensitivity. The tragedy of the common people is powerfully portrayed in these stories through the disintegration of individual psyches when political decisions are suddenly thrust upon them. Sympathy is evoked for the helplessness of the victim as well as the aggressor, both of whom are caught in the collapse of reason when they are wrenched away from the physical and psychological securities that have been built over generations. Derision, bewilderment and madness take over, and the boundary between the madhouse and the outside world collapses. In 'Toba Tek Singh' the absurdity of the madmen appears to be humane and reasonable when set against the bizarre scenes of rape, massacre and plunder that were witnessed during the Partition. Madness in the story is perhaps then a metaphor for sanity. The directness of the narration in the original story is rather deceptive, for it is a highly effective means of communicating its intricate complexity of theme and tone. The underlying irony and the black humour of the medley scenes of the mental asylum are woven smoothly into the texture of the story. The translator is faced with the challenge of recreating the absurdity of the situation without making it appear ludicrous. There are at least five different translations in English, and each attempts to render the original experience of the story in its own way.

TOBA TEK SINGH

A couple of years after Partition it struck the Governments of Pakistan and Hindustan that even as they had exchanged ordinary prisoners, so they should have an exchange of madmen as well. That is to say, the Muslim madmen who were lodged in the madhouses of Hindustan should be delivered to Pakistan, and the Hindu and Sikh madmen in the madhouses of Pakistan should be handed over to Hindustan.

One does not know if this was the right thing to do. Anyhow, as decided by those who know best, some high-level meetings were held on both sides of the border and a date was fixed for the exchange of madmen. The whole matter was thoroughly gone into. Such Muslim madmen as had their families still living in Hindustan were allowed to stay there, and all the rest were to be dispatched to the border. Here in Pakistan, as nearly all the Hindus and Sikhs had gone across anyhow, the question didn't arise of letting anyone stay; all the Hindu and Sikh madmen were escorted to the border under police guard.

This translation, which was first published in *Breakthrough,* a collection of modern Hindi and Urdu stories, edited by Sukrita Paul Kumar (Shimla: Indian Institute of Advanced Study, 1993), has been revised by the translator for this anthology.

One does not know what went on over there, but when the news of the exchange reached the madhouse here in Lahore, it gave rise to some highly interesting speculation. There was a Muslim madman who had been religiously reading *The Zamindar* for the previous dozen years. When he was asked by a friend, 'Maulvi Saheb, what is Pakistan?' he answered after much reflection, 'It's a place in Hindustan where they make cut-throat razors.'

This answer quite satisfied his friend.

In a similar vein, one Sikh madman asked another, 'Sardarji, why are we being sent to Hindustan? We can't even speak their language.'

The other one smiled. 'But I can speak the language of Hindustan—of the Hindustanis who are devilishly naughty and strut around all the time.'

One day while bathing, a Muslim madman shouted the slogan, 'Pakistan Zindabad' so lustily that he slipped and fell and quite passed out.

There were some madmen who weren't actually mad. Most of them were murderers whose families had bribed the officials concerned and fixed it up for these men to be sent to a madhouse rather than to the gallows. Now these madmen had some hazy notion why Hindustan had been partitioned and Pakistan created, but even they did not know anything like the whole truth. The newspapers never told one anything, and the policemen on guard were all illiterate and stupid so that one could make out precious little from hearing them talk. All that the madmen could be sure of was that there was a person called Mohammad Ali Jinnah, who was also known as Qaid-e-Azam, the Great Leader, and he had created a separate nation for the Musalmans which was called Pakistan. As to where it was and what its geographical dimensions were, they hadn't a clue. That being so, all the madmen in the madhouse who weren't completely mad were in some perplexity as to whether they were in Pakistan or in Hindustan. If they were in Hindustan, then where was this Pakistan, and if they were in Pakistan, then how was it that a little while ago, though staying in the very same place, they had been in Hindustan?

In fact one madman got caught up so badly in this whole confusion of Pakistan and Hindustan and Hindustan and Pakistan that he ended up considerably madder than before. While sweeping the yard one day he went and climbed up a tree and sitting on a branch delivered a two-hour lecture on the most ticklish matter of Pakistan and Hindustan. When the guards told him to get down he only climbed up a little further. When they shouted and threatened him he said, 'I want to live in neither Hindustan nor Pakistan. I had rather live on this tree.' After much ado, when he had cooled off, he climbed down and hugged all his Hindu and Sikh friends and began to cry. His heart grew heavy at the very thought that they would leave him and go away to Hindustan.

A radio engineer with an M.Sc. degree, who was a Musalman, kept apart from all the other madmen and was in the habit of walking quietly on a particular path in the garden all day long. The change now wrought in him was that he took off all his clothes and handed them over to the guards and began walking stark naked all over the garden.

A fat Musalman madman from Chiniot, who had been an active member of the Muslim League and who used to bathe some fifteen or sixteen times a day now suddenly gave up this practice. His name was Muhammad Ali. So he announced one day to all others in his barred enclosure that he was indeed Mohammad Ali Jinnah, the Qaid-e-Azam. Following his example, a Sikh madman promptly turned into Master Tara Singh. As bloodshed in that enclosure seemed imminent, each of these madmen was declared dangerous and removed to solitary cells.

There was a young Hindu lawyer from Lahore who had gone mad out of unrequited love. He grew very melancholy when he learnt that Amritsar had gone to Hindustan, for it was a Hindu girl from that town whom he had fallen in love with, and though she had spurned him, he had even in his madness been unable to forget her. So he heartily abused all the Hindu and Muslim leaders who had got together to have Hindustan divided. His beloved was a Hindustani and he had now become a Pakistani. When the business of exchange came up other madmen told the lawyer to take heart, for he would now be sent to Hindustan—to the Hindustan where his beloved was. But the lawyer did not wish to leave Lahore. He was afraid he might not be able to build up much of a legal practice in Amritsar.

In the European Ward there were two Anglo-Indian madmen. When they found out that the English had granted India freedom and gone home, they went into a deep depression. They spent hours secretly confabulating about what their status would now be in the madhouse. Would the European Ward be retained or be abolished? Would they get a proper English breakfast any more or not? Would they be served bread or would they be obliged to swallow the 'bloody Indian chapati'?

There was a Sikh who had been in the madhouse now for some fifteen years. Strange words were to be heard rolling off his tongue all the time: 'Opar di rumble-tumble di annexe of the thoughtless of the green lentils of the lantern.' He slept neither day nor night. The guards said he had not slept a wink all these fifteen years. He never even lay down. All he might do sometimes was to take a '*tek*', or lean his back against a wall. Because he stood all the time his feet were swollen and his calves were distended but in spite of the physical discomfort he never lay down to rest. He listened attentively whenever there was a discussion among the madmen on Hindustan, Pakistan and their own transfer from the one to the other. Whenever anyone asked him for his opinion he replied with the utmost seriousness: 'Opar di rumble-tumble di annexe of the thoughtless of the green lentils of the Government of Pakistan.' But later 'of the Government of Pakistan' was replaced by 'of the Government of Toba Tek Singh', and the other madmen began to ask him where this Toba Tek Singh was, and was that where he came from. But not one of them seemed to know whether it was in Pakistan or Hindustan. Whoever attempted to explain soon enough got confounded by the fact that Sialkot which had earlier been in Hindustan was now by all accounts in Pakistan. Who knew if Lahore which was now in Pakistan might not the very next day go over to Hindustan or the whole of Hindustan indeed become one vast Pakistan. And who could ever be sure and swear with his hand on his heart if both Hindustan and Pakistan might not one day disappear all together.

The Sikh madman had only a few sparse hair left. As he rarely bathed and the hair on his head and his beard had all got tangled together, he looked a fright. But never had this man done anyone any harm; he had never once got into a scrap in all his fifteen years. The older staff in the madhouse recalled that he had owned a great deal of landed property in Toba Tek Singh. He had been a well

off landlord when suddenly one day his brain tripped. His family had tied him up in heavy chains and come and got him locked up in the madhouse. Once a month they would come to visit him and inquire after his well-being. This arrangement had lasted for a long while but when all this trouble began about Hindustan and Pakistan their visits had come to an end.

His name was Bishan Singh but everyone called him Toba Tek Singh. He seldom seemed to know which day of the week it was or which month of the year or how many years had gone by. But he always knew unprompted and exactly when it was time for his family to come and visit. So he would tell a guard in advance that his visitors were on the way. On that day he would give himself a good scrub and soap himself all over and oil his hair and nicely comb it. He would call for his own clothes, which he never wore on any other occasion, and go to meet his visitors all dressed up. If they asked him anything he would either keep quiet or sometimes say, 'Opar di rumble-tumble di annexe of the thoughtless of the green lentils of the lantern.'

He had a daughter who had been growing by a finger's width each passing month until at fifteen years of age she was a proper young woman. Bishan Singh did not know her at all when he saw her. She had cried at the sight of her father when she was a little infant. Now that she was grown up her eyes still flowed with tears.

When the matter of Pakistan and Hindustan arose he began to ask other madmen where Toba Tek Singh was. At getting no satisfactory reply his itch for an answer grew worse by the day. Now he had no visitors either. Earlier he had always known when a visit was coming up, but now it was as if the voice of his heart which had earlier signalled their visits to him had fallen silent. He wished very much that those who used to bring him sympathy and fruits and sweets and clothes would come. If only he could ask them where Toba Tek Singh was! They would surely have told him if it was in Pakistan or Hindustan, for he was sure that they themselves were from Toba Tek Singh where his lands were.

There was in the madhouse a man who called himself Khuda,

namely God. When Bishan Singh asked him one day if Toba Tek Singh was in Pakistan or Hindustan, he first gave a loud guffaw, as was his wont, and then said, 'It is in neither Pakistan nor Hindustan, for we haven't passed our orders yet!'

Bishan Singh pleaded with this God time and again and implored him to pass his orders so that the matter might be resolved once and for all, but he was very busy as he had numerous other orders to pass as well. One day in the end Bishan Singh lost his temper with him and burst out, 'Opar di rumble-tumble di annexe of the thoughtless of the green lentils of Vahe Guruji da Khalsa and Vahe Guruji di Fateh and God bless him who says Sat Sri Akal!' What he probably meant to say was that this God was the God of the Musalmans and would surely have heeded him had he been the God of the Sikhs instead.

A few days before the exchange, an old Musalman friend of his from Toba Tek Singh came to visit. He had never been to visit before. Bishan Singh had one look at him and turned to go back in. But the guards stopped him. 'This is your friend Fazaldin, and he has come to see you.'

Bishan Singh gave Fazaldin a look and began to mutter something. Fazaldin came up and placed a hand on his shoulder. 'I had been meaning for a long time to come and see you, but couldn't find the time. All your folk were able safely to go over to Hindustan. I did whatever I could to help them. Your daughter... Roop Kaur...' He hesitated and stopped.

Bishan Singh tried to remember, 'Daughter? Roop Kaur?'

Fazaldin haltingly added, 'Yes, she too... is very well... She too had gone away with them.'

Bishan Singh kept quiet. Fazaldin spoke again. 'They had asked me to come and look you up from time to time. Now I hear you are off to Hindustan. Say my salaam to dear brethren Balbir Singh and Vadhava Singh, and to sister Amrit Kaur. Tell brother Balbir Singh that Fazaldin is well. The two brown buffaloes they had left me have both delivered, one a male calf and the other a female, but the female died on the sixth day. And...well, do let me know if there's anything I can do; I am always at your service... And here, I have brought you some home-made sweets.'

Bishan Singh took the bag of sweets, passed it on to the guard standing beside them, and asked Fazaldin, 'Where is Toba Tek Singh?'

'Toba Tek Singh?' he answered with some surprise. 'What do you mean, where is Toba Tek Singh? Well, it's right where it always was.'

Bishan Singh asked, 'In Pakistan or in Hindustan?'

'In Hindustan—no, no, I mean, in Pakistan,' Fazaldin said, as if out of his wits.

Bishan Singh went away muttering, 'Opar di rumble-tumble di annexe of the thoughtless of the green lentils of Pakistan and Hindustan and shame on the lot of you!'

The arrangements for the exchange were all complete. Lists of the madmen to be sent over there from over here and over here from over there had been exchanged and the date of the transfer been fixed. It was bitterly cold. Police vans full of Hindu and Sikh madmen departed from the madhouse of Lahore, escorted by the officers concerned. At the border at Wagah the respective superintendents of police met and after the necessary preliminaries the exchange commenced and went on all night.

It was no easy task to bring the madmen out of the vans and to hand them over to the other set of officials. Some would not budge at all, and others who did come out ran off in all directions. Those who were naked tore off any clothes which the officers attempted to put on them. Some shouted abuse and some sang. Some wept and some howled with misery. It was difficult to hear oneself speak. Mad women made their own din too and it was so bitterly cold as to make one's teeth chatter.

Most of the madmen had not wanted this transfer. They could not understand why they were being uprooted and thrown out. Some who could reason and think a little were raising slogans of 'Pakistan Zindabad!' and 'Pakistan Murdabad!' This all but led to a riot, since these slogans roused the passions of some Muslims and Sikhs.

When it was Bishan Singh's turn and the concerned official from across Wagah began to write down his name in his register, he asked, 'Where is Toba Tek Singh? In Pakistan or in Hindustan?'

The official laughed and said, 'In Pakistan.'

Bishan Singh at once sprang up and ran back to where the rest of his friends were. The Pakistani policeman caught hold of him and tried to lead him across to the other side but he refused to go with them. 'Toba Tek Singh is here…!' he began to shout at the top of his voice, 'Opar di rumble-tumble di annexe of the thoughtless of the green lentils of Toba Tek Singh and Pakistan…'

They tried their best to coax and cajole him, 'Look, Toba Tek Singh has now gone to Hindustan—and even if it hasn't yet we shall arrange very soon to send it there.' But he was unmoved. When they tried to take him across forcibly he went and stood on his swollen legs at a spot in the middle with an air that suggested that no one could now remove him from there. As he seemed a harmless enough fellow they did not use undue force, and he was allowed to stand there while the rest of the proceedings went on.

Just before dawn a cry that rent the air came out of Bishan Singh who still stood stock-still. Several officers came running up and found that the man who had stood on his legs day and night for all of fifteen years was now lying on his face. Over there behind the barbed wire fence lay Hindustan and over here behind the barbed wire fence lay Pakistan. In the middle on a strip of no man's land lay Toba Tek Singh.

Translated from the Urdu
by Harish Trivedi

ANNOTATIONS

Title: 'Toba Tek Singh is indeed the name of a small town in Pakistan, about 150 kms south-west of Lahore' (translator's note). According to the *Punjab Gazetteer* of 1907, it was named 'after a chaprasi who turned a fakir and made a tank there' (p. 152).

Page 106
The Zamindar: An Urdu daily." *Maulvi Saheb:* A scholar in religious studies. *the language of Hindustan:* Khalid Hasan, in his translation of the story, retains the word 'Hindostoros', used in the original Urdu, for 'Hindustan', perhaps to evoke the tone of derision suggested by the corruption of 'Hindustan' *(Mottled Dawn,* Penguin, 1997). *Mohammad Ali Jinnah:* (1876–1948), popularly known as Qaid-e-Azam (the great leader) and recognized as the founder of Pakistan. He was President of the Muslim League and the first

Governor-General of Pakistan. He promulgated the Pakistan Ordinance in 1948 to implement an agreement with India regarding the exchange of prisoners.

Page 107
Chiniot: A place in Kashmir.
the Muslim League: The All India Muslim League was founded in 1906 as the representative organization of the Indian Muslims. The Congress and the League were the principal political organizations of India before the Partition. In 1940, the Muslim League passed the Pakistan Resolution which provided for a separate state for Muslims.
Master Tara Singh: One of the most powerful Akali Sikh leaders at the time of the Partition. Since he was a popular teacher the title of 'master' stayed with his name. He raised the formal demand for a sovereign Sikh nation in 1944, when the creation of Pakistan seemed inevitable.

Page 108
Opar di rumble-tumble di...lantern: This gibberish in the original Urdu is: 'Opar di gur gur di annexe di bedhyana di moong di daal di of di laltain'. Most translators retain the original while Harish Trivedi translates some words into English. The gibberish is a mix of sense and nonsense and it acquires different shades of meaning as the story progresses. Some words get changed, added or deleted each time it is uttered.
take a 'tek': The other translations of the story do not retain the word *'tek'* from the original Urdu. The translator has retained it here perhaps because he wishes to suggest a connection with Toba Tek Singh's name.

Page 110
Vahe Guruji da Khalsa: 'Vahe Guruji' is God, the highest truth that triumphs through his Khalsa. The Khalsa is 'God's own force'. The Khalsas are the 'saint' soldiers who stand for the purest form of truth.
Vahe Guruji di Fateh: 'God is victorious'.
Sat Sri Akal: 'Truth is eternal'; a form of greeting among Sikhs.
brethren... sister: These kinship terms ('Bhai' and 'Bahan' in the original) suggest the closeness that Fazaldin feels towards his Hin-

du friends. It is customary among the Sikhs to address a man as 'Bhai' and a woman as 'Bahan', as in the original Urdu: 'Bhai Balbir Singh', 'Bhai Vadhava Singh', and 'Bahan Amrit Kaur'.

Page 111
Opar di... the lot of you: The gibberish in the original here is: 'Opar di gur gur di annexe di bedhyana di moong di daal of di Pakistan and Hindustan of di dur fitey munh'.
Wagah: The territory of Pakistan ends at the border at Wagah.

Page 112
Over there... Toba Tek Singh: The last sentence of the story is translated by Tahira Naqvi as follows: 'In the middle, on a stretch of land which had no name, lay Toba Tek Singh' *(Stories About the Partition of India,* ed. Alok Bhalla, vol. 3, New Delhi: HarperCollins, 1994).

SUGGESTED READING

Bhalla, Alok ed., *The Life and Works of Saadat Hasan Manto,* Shimla: Indian Institute of Advanced Study, 1997.

Flemming, Leslie A., *Another Lonely Voice: The Life and Works of Saadat Hasan Manto,* Lahore: Vanguard, 1985.

Kumar, Sukrita Paul, 'Literary Modernism and Some Partition Stories', *The New Story,* Shimla: Indian Institute of Advanced Study in association with Allied Publishers, New Delhi, 1990.

Manto, Saadat Hasan, *Partition: Sketches and Stories,* trans, and ed. Khalid Hasan, New Delhi: Viking, 1991.

Wadhavan, Jagdish Chander, *Manto Naama: The Life of Saadat Hasan Manto,* trans. Jai Ratan, New Delhi: Roli Books, 1998.

ISMAT CHUGHTAI

(1915–91)

Ismat Khanum Chughtai was born in Badayun (Uttar Pradesh) in a large middle class Muslim household. A rebel right from her childhood days, she was more interested in the activities of boys than in the conventional pastimes of girls of her age. It was her eldest brother, Azim Beg Chughtai, also a writer, who encouraged her to read. Born in an age when girls, especially Muslim girls, were discouraged from studying, she had to overcome many challenges before she got her BA and BT (Bachelor of Teaching) degrees. She worked as head mistress of various schools in Rajasthan and Uttar Pradesh, and later as Superintendent of Schools in Bombay. In 1942 she married her long-standing friend, Shahid Lateef, a film director. In 1943 she gave up her job for a full-time career in writing and a long association with the film world. *Garam Hawa,* a film based on one of her stories, received the National Award for the best film on national integration for the year 1973. Among various other awards, she received the Padmashree in 1975 for her versatile contribution to Urdu Literature. She died on 24 October 1991 in Bombay. Even in her death she was dogged by controversies when, according to her wishes, she was cremated instead of being buried in the traditional Muslim manner.

Chughtai began her career at a time when women wrote in the romantic and sentimental vein. However, she was influenced by the realism of Russian Literature, and by the radicalism of Rashid Jahan, the bold and revolutionary Urdu writer. Although Chughtai was briefly associated with the Progressive Writers' Movement, she was never confined within the narrow definitions of organized movements. Yet she displays a deep sympathy for the oppressed and her writing presents a radicalism that strikes at the very roots of society. Most of her stories revolve around the exploitation of women and their economic and psychological problems. Her novel *Terhi Lakir* (The Crooked Line, 1943) is a portrayal of the vicissitudes

that a girl faces when she tries to live her life on her own terms. Chughtai also successfully captures the vanishing world of Muslim middle class India, hitting out ruthlessly at its hypocrisies, its hollow religiosity, its superstitions and ritualism, its contradictions and double standards. The unconventionality of Chughtai's themes is matched by powerful narration. Varying her tone between sympathy and irony, she manages to find a narrative style that is balanced between humour and cruelty. Rejecting the ornamental feminine style of her predecessors, Chughtai developed an individual, colloquial one, using the simple, earthy language of the common people, especially women, with its curses and abuses, its special turns of phrase and idioms, its metaphors and similies. This colloquial style is very difficult to capture in translation.

Some of Chughtai's better known works are her novels, *Masooma* (The Innocent Girl, 1964) and *Ziddi* (Stubborn, 1940): and *Chui Mui* (Touch-Me-Not, 1952) which is a collection of short stories. Chughtai's first story, *Gainda* (Marigold) was published in 1939 in *Saaqi,* an Urdu magazine. Her boldness in probing the harsh realities of her social milieu prompted readers to assume that it was a man writing under the name of a woman. When *Lihaf* (The Quilt) was published in *Adab-e-Latif* in 1942, it immediately created a furore and Chughtai had to face extremely hostile reactions. For a long time she had to struggle with the label of obscenity and was dismissed as someone who wrote only about sex. She was even charged with obscenity by the Imperial Crown Court in 1944. The judge, however, did not find the story to be obscene and the charge was dropped. This early notoriety was very hard to live down for Chughtai. It was her economic security based on her comfortable earnings in the film world, combined with her persistence, that enabled her to continue writing, despite the reluctance of the critics to evaluate and accept her.

'Lihaf' deals with sexual frustrations and unconventional sexual relations. It is the story of Begum Jan who is a victim of social circumstances, and of a young, precocious girl who attempts to come to grips with a reality that she cannot understand. The 'quilt' in the title is a metaphor for secrecy and concealment as well as a trope for the narrative. The writer uses the consciousness of the young girl to present a situation which is never spelled out but is nevertheless conveyed in all its complexity to the

reader. What the adult writer wants to communicate about the relationship being conducted under the quilt is concealed by the bewilderment of the young narrator and we see only its frightening shadow.

LIHAF (THE QUILT)

Every winter when I pull the lihaf over me, and the shadow it casts on the wall sways like an elephant, with a sudden bound my mind begins to race and scour over the past. What memories revive in me!

I don't propose here to tell you a romantic tale about my own lihaf. Indeed, no romance can be properly associated with a lihaf. Come to think of it, a blanket may be less comfortable, but its shadow is never so frightening... as the rocking shadow of a lihaf on the wall. My story dates from the days when I was very young and used to spend the whole day getting into fights with my brothers and their male friends. I sometimes wonder why the devil was I so quarrelsome in those days. At the age when the other girls were securing admirers, I was busy fighting every boy or girl that came my way.

That was the reason why, when Mother went on a visit to Agra, she left me for a week in the care of her adopted sister. Mother knew very well that there wasn't a single child, not even a mouse of a one, to quarrel with in that house. A nice punishment for me! Well, so it came about that I was left with Begum Jan, the same Begum Jan whose lihaf has burnt itself into my memory and is to this day preserved in it like a scar from a red-hot iron. Begum Jan's poor parents had given her in marriage to the Nawab Sahib because, although somewhat 'advanced' in age, the Nawab was a very pious man. No prostitute or street woman had ever been seen in his house. He had gone on the hajj pilgrimage to Mecca himself, and had helped many others to perform this holy service.

But the Nawab had a mysterious hobby. It is common for people to have a craze for pigeons or for cock fights and so on. The Nawab detested such silly interests. His only pleasure was to have students around him, young, fair-faced boys with slim waists, whose expenses were generously borne by the Nawab Sahib himself.

After marrying Begum Jan, and installing her in his house along with the furniture, the Nawab Sahib totally forgot her presence, leaving the frail young Begum to pine in loneliness.

It is difficult to say where Begum Jan's life begins; at the point when she made the first mistake of stepping into this world, or when she became the wife of a nawab and was tethered to her canopied bed; or when the boys invaded the Nawab Sahib's life and sumptuous dishes and rich sweets began to be prepared for him, and she felt she was rolling on a bed of live coals as she watched from the chinks in the drawing room door and saw the boys in their translucent *kurtas,* their well-formed legs in tight-fitting *churidars,* their willowy waists… or, does it begin when all her prayers and vows, her vigils and charms failed to move the Nawab? What's the use of applying leeches to a stone? The Nawab didn't budge an inch. When this happened Begum Jan was heartbroken. She turned to books. But this too failed. Romantic novels and sentimental poetry left her even more dejected. She lost sleep and became a bundle of regret and despondence.

To hell with all those clothes! One dresses up in fine clothes to catch another's eye. But here, neither did the Nawab Sahib have any time to spare from the boys to look at her, nor did he let her go visit other people. Ever since she had been married, Begum Jan's relatives had come to visit her, staying for months, while the poor lady herself never escaped the confinement of her house. Those relatives made her blood boil. They all came to enjoy themselves, eat the rich food that the Nawab Sahib served, and have their winter needs provided for, while she would lie in the cold, feeling chilly even under her lihaf, freshly stuffed with cotton which had been teased out into a fluff. As she turned in her bed, the lihaf threw ever-changing shadows on the wall, but not one of these held any hope or solace for her. Why should one live then?… Well, one lives as long as life lasts. It was in her stars that she should live, and live she did.

It was Rabbu who pulled her back from the brink. And then in no time, Begum Jan's dried-up body began to fill, her cheeks glowed, her beauty burst into bloom. The massage of a mysterious oil brought back the flush of life to her. And the best medical journals, if you ask me, will not give the prescription for this oil.

When I first saw Begum Jan she must have been forty or forty-two. How elegantly she reclined on the *masnad,* with Rabbu sitting close and kneading her back and her body! She had thrown a purple shawl across her legs and looked as grand as a queen. I was quite enamored of her looks. I was happy to sit near her and look at her for hours. Her dark, luxuriously oiled hair was neatly parted, and so immaculately set that not a strand of hair could be found straying. Her eyes were black and her carefully plucked eyebrows were like drawn bows. Her eyes were a little distended with heavy eyelids and thick lashes. But it was her lips, often reddened, that were the most amazingly attractive feature of her face. She had a downy upper lip with the faint suggestion of a mustache. Her hair grew long at her temples. Sometimes watching her face you had the queer feeling that you were looking at the face of a young boy.

Her skin was white and smooth as though someone had stitched it tightly on her body. Often when she uncovered her legs below the knees so that she could scratch them, I would cast sneaking glances to see how they glistened. She had a tall figure and, being well clothed with flesh, she looked large of build. But her body was perfectly molded and beautifully proportionate. She had large, white, smooth hands and a well-formed waistline. Well then, as I was saying, Rabbu used to sit with her, scratching her back. She sat for hours doing it, as if scratching the back was one of the basic necessities of life, perhaps even more than a basic necessity.

Rabbu had no other job assigned to her. She sat all the time with Begum Jan, on the canopied bed, massaging her legs or her head or various other parts of her body. It bewildered me sometimes to watch the endless kneading and rubbing. I can't speak for others, but I can say that my body would have disintegrated under so much pounding. And this vigorous daily massaging was not all. On the day Begum Jan took her bath the ritual became more elaborate. God, to think of it! For two full hours before she entered the bath, she would have her body rubbed with all kinds of oils, perfumed unguents, and lotions. That would go on so long that the very thought of it made my imagination race. The doors of her room were shut, the braziers were lighted, and the massage would begin. Generally only Rabbu was in the room with her. The other maids stood by at the door, murmuring and handing in whatever was required.

The fact is that Begum Jan suffered from a permanent itch. Hundreds of oils and unguents were tried but the poor woman could not get rid of it. The doctors and hakims said there was nothing they could diagnose. The skin lay clean, without a blemish. If there was a disorder below the skin they wouldn't know. 'Oh these wretched doctors, they are so stupid! Who would believe you have a disease? Your blood, God bless you, is a little heated, that's all,' Rabbu says smiling and looks at Begum Jan with her eyes screwed into a slit. As for this Rabbu—she was as dark-skinned as Begum Jan was fair, as flushed in her face as Begum Jan was snowy white. She seemed to glow like heated iron. There were faint pockmarks on her face. She had a robust, solid body, small, nimble hands, a small, taut belly and fat, always moist, lips. Her body exuded a distracting odor. How quick her small, plump hands were! This moment you saw them at Begum Jan's waist and in a trice they were at her thighs and then racing down to her ankles. As for me, I used to watch those hands whenever I sat near Begum Jan, intent on seeing where they were and what they were doing.

Winter or summer, Begum Jan always wore fine-spun Hyderabadi lace kurtas, foamy white over her dark colored pajamas. The fan was kept going as a rule. Begum Jan habitually draped a light shawl over her body. She loved the winter months. I enjoyed staying with her in winter. She avoided exertion. One always found her lying relaxed on the carpet, munching dry fruit, while her back was being scratched. The other maids in the house held a bitter grudge against Rabbu. The witch!

She ate with Begum Jan, was her constant companion, and even slept with her! Rabbu and Begum Jan were a topic of amused conversation at social functions and gatherings. There were bursts of laughter the moment their names were mentioned. Innumerable stories had been coined about the poor lady. She, on her part, never stirred out, never met anyone. It was just herself and her itch, and the world could go by! As I was telling you, I was a small girl at the time I am talking about and was quite enamored of Begum Jan. She, too, was very fond of me. And that is why, when Mother went to Agra, knowing that left by myself in the house I would run wild and start up a war with my brothers, she left me for a week with Begum Jan. It delighted me and Begum Jan alike. After all, she had declared herself my mother's sister.

Where was I to sleep? Naturally, in Begum Jan's room. So a small cot was placed for me next to Begum Jan's bedstead. On that first night, Begum Jan and I chatted and played 'Chance' till ten or eleven. Then I went over to my bed to sleep. When I fell asleep, Rabbu was still with Begum Jan, scratching her back as usual. The low woman! I thought.

Sometime in the night I suddenly woke up, feeling a strange kind of dread. The room was in total darkness, and in the darkness Begum Jan's lihaf was rocking as though an elephant were caught in it.

'Begum Jan—,' I called out timidly. The elephant stopped moving. The lihaf subsided. 'What is it?—Go to sleep—,' came Begum Jan's voice, from somewhere.

'I feel frightened—,' I said in a scared, mousy voice. 'Go to sleep—what's there to frighten you—just say the "Aayat-al-Kursi".'

'Okay.' I started repeating the 'Aayat-al-Kursi' hurriedly but got stuck in the middle although I knew it by heart quite well. 'May I come over to you, Begum Jan?'

'No, daughter,—get back to sleep.' This a little sternly. And then' I heard two people whispering. Dear me! Who was this other one? I felt even more scared.

'Begum Jan—do you think there is a thief around?'

'Get to sleep, girl—what thief could there be?' This was Rabbu's voice. I quickly pulled my head back under my lihaf and went back to sleep.

By next morning the whole frightening scene had vanished from my mind. I've always been of an apprehensive nature. When I was a child, I had nightmares. Muttering in my sleep, waking up suddenly, and bolting from the bed were daily occurrences. People said I was possessed. The previous night's incident, therefore, quite slipped from my mind. In the morning the lihaf looked absolutely innocent.

When I awoke on the second night, I felt as though a dispute between Rabbu and Begum Jan were being silently settled on the bed. I could not make out anything, nor could I tell how it was decided. I only heard Rabbu's convulsive sobs, then noises like those of a cat licking a plate, lap, lap. I was so frightened that I went back to sleep.

One day Rabbu went off to see her son, a perverse lad. Begum Jan had done a lot to help him. She had set up a shop for him, and tried to settle him in a village, but he was amenable to nothing. For a time, he too took up the service of the Nawab Sahib and received many gifts of clothes from him, but then, no one knew why, he fled and never turned up at the house even to see his mother. So Rabbu had to go to see him at a relative's. Begum Jan was unhappy about that, but Rabbu had no choice.

The whole day Begum Jan was disconsolate. Her body ached at every joint. She didn't want anyone to touch her. She didn't eat anything and was dejected the whole day long.

'Shall I scratch your back, Begum Jan?' I asked with eagerness, shuffling a pack of cards. Begum Jan looked at me intently.

'Shall I?... Really?' And I put the cards away.

For a while I did the scratching, and Begum Jan said nothing. She just lay quiet. The next day Rabbu should have returned, but she didn't. Begum Jan grew irritable—she drank several cups of tea and gave herself a headache.

Once again I sat scratching her back—smooth like a table top... I kept on gently scratching. One felt so happy doing something for her!

'A little harder—undo the buttons,' Begum Jan told me. 'This side—ah me, a little below the shoulder, here—yes—there's a nice girl!—Ah!—Ah!—,' she sighed with pleasure.

'Further, this side.' Begum Jan could have easily reached the spot with her own hand, but she was making me do it, and instead of resenting it, I felt important.

'Here,' She said. '—Oi,—you're tickling me.'

'—You!—' and she giggled. I had kept talking to her while I scratched.

'Tomorrow I'll send you out shopping,' she continued. 'What will you buy? A doll that opens and shuts its eyes again?'

'No, Begum Jan, not a doll. I'm not a child now.'

'What are you then, an old woman?' she laughed. 'All right, buy a *babua*—make the clothes yourself. I will give you lots of cloth to do it with.' She turned as she spoke.

'Fine,' I said.

'Here,' she took my hand and placed it where she felt the itching. She kept guiding my hand wherever she wanted to be

scratched, and I, lost in thinking of the babua, went on scratching mechanically while she kept up her chatter.

'Listen, you don't have many frocks left. Tomorrow I'll get the tailor to make a new one for you. Your mother has left some cloth with me.'

T don't want one of that red cloth… it looks cheap…' I was prattling and did not notice where my hand had wandered, nor that Begum Jan was now lying on her back, supine. 'Oh my…!' I hastily withdrew my hand.

'Dear me, child! Watch where you're scratching—you're tearing up my ribs,' Begum Jan said with a shy, mischievous smile, making me blush.

'Come here, lie down by my side.' And she made me lie down with my head resting on her arm.

'Dear, dear! How thin you are! All your ribs show.' She counted my ribs.

'Oo-oo!' I mumbled.

'Oui?—I wouldn't gobble you up, would I?—What a tight sweater! You haven't even put on a warm vest.' I began to fidget.

'How many ribs does one have?' She changed the tenor.

'Nine on one side and ten on the other,' I said, haphazardly recalling hygiene lessons learned at school.

'Let's see, take off your hand—right—one—two—three!' I wished desperately to escape but she held me tight and pressed me to herself.

'Ouh!' I protested—Begum Jan began to laugh loudly. Even now when I think of how she looked that day I feel quite distraught. Her heavy eyelids had grown heavier, the down on her upper lip darker, and, in spite of the chilly weather, tiny drops of sweat glistened on her lips and nose. Her hands were cold as ice but so soft that it felt as though the skin on them had been peeled off. She had taken off her shawl, and in her thin kurta her body gleamed like dough. Heavy gold studs that had come undone were swinging to one side of her open front. Dusk had fallen and the room was in total darkness. An unknown dread took hold of me. I felt bewildered. Begum Jan's eyes had deepened. I began to weep inwardly. She hugged and squeezed me like a plaything. The warmth of her body drove me to distraction. But she paid no

attention, she was like one possessed. And I could neither scream nor cry.

After a while she lay back exhausted. Her face grew dull and unattractive. She started taking long breaths. She is dying, I thought, and jumping up, took to my heels.

Rabbu, thank God, was back in the evening, and as I got into bed still nervous, I quickly pulled the quilt over me to sleep. But sleep wouldn't come and I lay awake for hours.

Why was Mother taking so long to return? Begum Jan so scared me now that I passed the whole day with the servants. The mere thought of setting foot in her room was enough to drive me out of my wits. There was no one I could speak my mind to. And what could I say, after all? That I was scared of Begum Jan, the Begum Jan who, everybody knew, was so fond of me?

Rabbu and Begum Jan had fallen out again, to my ill luck. This had me worried, for suddenly it occurred to Begum Jan that I was too much out of doors in the cold and would certainly catch pneumonia and die.

'Young girl!' she said. 'Do you want that my head should be shaved? If anything happened to you, I'd be held responsible.' She sat me down near her. She was washing herself in a basin placed before her and the tea was ready on a small table.

'Pour a cup out for yourself, and give me a cup too,' she said, drying her face on a towel. 'I'll get changed in the meantime.'

I sipped tea while she dressed. Whenever Begum Jan called me to her when her back was being rubbed, I would go, but keep my face averted and run back at the first chance. Now when she began changing in my presence the gorge rose in me. Looking away, I kept sipping my tea.

'Oh, Mother!' a voice within me called out in despair. 'Is quarrelling with one's brothers such an offense that you should cause me all this...' Mother was always against my playing with boys. As if boys were carnivorous beasts who would eat up her dear one. And what boys were they after all! My own brothers and a few of their rotten little friends. But Mother thought otherwise. For her, womankind had to be kept under lock and key. And here I was, more scared of Begum Jan than of all the loafers in the world. I would have run into the street that moment if I could. But I sat helpless.

After she had dressed, Begum Jan went through her elaborate toilet. When the makeup was over the warm scent of the perfumed oils she had used made her glow like an ember, and she prepared to shower her affection on me.

'I want to go home,' I repeated in reply to every proposal she made. And I started crying.

'Come, sit beside me,' she coaxed. 'I'll take you to the bazaar-listen to me...'

But I would have none of it. 'I want to go home' was my one response to all the toys and sweets that were being offered.

'Your brother will hit you when you are home, you little witch,' she said, slapping me affectionately.

'Let him beat me as much as he will,' I thought to myself and remained withdrawn and stiff.

'Unripe mangoes are sour, Begum Jan,' Rabbu offered acidly. And then, suddenly, Begum Jan had a fit. The gold necklace which a moment before she had wanted to put around my neck flew into pieces, her fine lace *dupatta* was in shreds, and the neat part in her hair, never for a moment disturbed, was all roughed up. 'Oh!— Oh! Oh! Oh!' she began to scream. Her body shook with convulsive jerks. I ran out of the room.

It was a long time before Begum Jan could calm down. When later I tiptoed into the bedroom, I found Rabbu sitting with her, massaging her body.

'Take your shoes off,' Rabbu said as she scratched Begum Jan's ribs. Like a frightened mouse I crept into my bed and pulled the lihaf over me.

Sr—sr—phat—kitch... In the darkness, Begum Jan's lihaf was swaying again like an elephant. 'My God,' I murmured, my voice faint with fear. The elephant leapt inside the lihaf, and then lay still. I was quiet. But the elephant was on the rampage again. I trembled from head to foot. I decided that I should gather all my courage and switch on the light at the head of the bed. The elephant rose, agitated. It seemed to be trying to sit on its legs. I heard noises, slop, slop—as if someone were eating something with great relish. Suddenly I understood the whole affair. Begum Jan hadn't eaten anything that day and Rabbu—Rabbu had always been a greedy glutton. Surely something delicious was being gulped down under the lihaf. I sniffed the air trying to catch the

aroma. Only the warm scent of attar, sandalwood, and henna

reached me.

The lihaf was swelling again. I did my best to lie still and ignore it. But the lihaf began to take on such strange, outlandish shapes that it sent shivers down my spine. It seemed like a huge, bloated frog inflating itself and about to spring on me. I plucked up the courage to make some disturbing noises, but no one took notice and the lihaf entered my skull and began to swell there. Hesitatingly I brought my legs down on the other side of the bed, groped for the switch and pressed the button. Under the lihaf the elephant turned a violent somersault and collapsed. But the somersault had lifted the corner of the lihaf by a foot—'Allah!' I dived for my bed!

Translated from the Urdu
by Syed Sirajuddin

ANNOTATIONS

Title: Lihaf: A thick quilt.

Page 117
male friends: The word 'friend' in English is gender non-specific, while 'dost', the Urdu word in the original text, is gender specific—'a male friend'.
when the other girls were securing admirers: The Urdu word for 'admirers' in the original is 'ashique'. When Chughtai was on trial for obscenity, the prosecution had a difficult time locating specific instances. The best they could do was to pick out this phrase. Their argument was that girls from respectable families do not 'collect admirers'. The judge, however, was not convinced and the charge was dropped.
adopted sister: This seems to be the closest translation of the phrase in Urdu, 'muhboli bahan', but it does not quite convey the original meaning. 'Adopted' implies a legal status, while 'muhboli' is an informal acknowledgement of a sisterly bond. *Begum Jan:* Begum Jan was based on a real life character. Years later, when Chughtai happened to meet her, she was delighted to know that the lady had divorced her husband, had remarried, and had given birth to a son. Chughtai wrote in her autobiography that she had long wanted

some bold young man to rescue Begum Jan from the clutches of the witch Rabbu *(Kaaghazi Hai Pairahan*
[The Apparel is Paper-Thin], Delhi: Raj Kamal Prakashan, 1998, pp. 42–3).
bajj... Mecca: see note on 'The Holy Panchayat', p. 65.

Page 118
along with the furniture: The original phrase, 'kul saazo samaan ke saath' translates as 'along with all his possessions'. *was tethered to her canopied bed:* 'tethered' for 'zindagi guzarne lagi' seems too strong a word. The strength of Chughtai's style is the simplicity of her statements, without any loaded meanings, in spite of which her ideological viewpoint comes across with great force. A more apt translation would be: 'began to spend her life on the canopied bed'.
rich sweets began to be prepared for him: It is not 'him' but 'them'. The confusion arises from the Urdu word 'unke' which means both 'him' and 'them'. But in the context here 'them' is more appropriate, for it was the students who were being pampered thus.
churidars: close-fitting pajamas with lots of pleats near the ankles.
applying leeches to a stone: In the medieval system of medicine leeches were applied to the human body to suck out blood as a means of curing many ailments. The phrase here emphasizes the futility of Begum Jan's efforts to get the Nawab's attention. *The Nawab didn't budge an inch. When this happened...:* A better construction would be: 'When the Nawab didn't budge an inch, Begum Jan was...'
the best medical journals: The original does not have 'medical'.

Page 119
masnad: a bolster.
and look at her for hours: A sentence has been omitted after this: 'She was absolutely fair—there was not even a hint of rosiness'. *murmuring and handing in...:* 'Muttering' would be a more appropriate translation of 'badbadaati', the word used in the original.

Page 120
your blood...is a little heated: 'khoon mein garmi hai'. Syeda Hameed's translation is more appropriate here: 'It is your hot blood that causes all the trouble!' *(The Quilt and Other Stories,* p. 11).

Page 121

the 'Aayat-al-Kursi': A verse from the Quran recited to ward off evil.

Page 122

shuffling a pack of cards: A more accurate translation is 'dealing the cards'.

babua: A male doll.

Page 123

Begum Jan said with a shy mischievous smile: 'shy' seems to be a misprint for 'sly' here.

Page 125

dupatta: a veil or a scarf which covers the head and is wrapped around the shoulders.

Page 126

'Allah!' I dived for my bed: The ending in Syeda Hameed's translation is as follows: 'Allah! I dove headlong into my sheets!! What I saw when the quilt was lifted, I will never tell anyone, not even if they give me a lakh of rupees'. This is how the story ended when it first appeared in 1942, in *Adab-e-Latif* and in a collection of Chughtai's short stories. However, when Saadat Hasan Manto read the story he remarked: '…but the last line is not artistic at all. Had I been the editor in place of Ahmad Nadeem, I would certainly have deleted it. So when I spoke to Ismat about the story I said: "I liked your 'Lihaf very much. It is truly the distinctive feature of your style to use words in a judiciously economical fashion. But I was surprised that you wrote a pointless sentence at the end of your story"'. Subsequently, the story was published without the last sentence (Manto, 'Ismat Chughtai', in *Naye Adab Maymar,* Bombay: Qutb Publishers, 1948).

SUGGESTED READING

Chughtai, Ismat, *The Quilt & Other Stories,* trans. Tahira Naqvi and Syeda S. Hameed, Delhi: Kali for Women, 1990.

Kumar, Sukrita Paul and Sadiq eds, *Ismat: The Life and Times of Ismat Chughtai,* New Delhi: Katha, 1999.

Tharu, Susie & K. Lalita eds, *Women Writing in India: 600 BC to the Present,* vol. 2, New Delhi: Oxford University Press, 1993, Introduction and pp. 126–9.

Ambai
(b. 1944)

C. S. Lakshmi (Ambai) inherited her love of the Tamil language and culture from her self-taught grandmother and her mother—a musician who sang Tamil lyrics and subscribed to popular Tamil journals. She borrowed her pen-name from Devan's novel *Parvatiyin Sangalpam* (Parvati's Vow), in which the protagonist, Parvati, deserted by her husband on account of her 'inferior intelligence', begins writing under the pseudonym 'Ambai' and becomes famous. Later, when her husband wishes to return to her, she rejects him. C. S. Lakshmi was so impressed by this character's determination that she chose Ambai as her pen-name when she began writing in her teens. Two of Ambai's novels were published before she was twenty. She also gave performances of classical music and dance until 1974. She taught for a while at a college in Delhi and completed her doctorate in American history from Jawaharlal Nehru University. Besides novels, Ambai has published two collections of short stories; she has also written plays and scripts for films. Her first collection of short stories, *Siragugal Muriyum* (Wings Get Broken), published in 1976, is an important milestone in the history of women's writing in Tamil. She was a regular contributor to the literary journal *Kanaiyazhi* (The Signet Ring), and was actively associated with *Pregnyai* (Consciousness). She is married to the film-maker Vishnu Mathur, and lives in Mumbai. Ambai has worked on the social history of women in Tamil Nadu and on Dalit writers and women activists. Her three-volume study of the lives of women artists of Tamil Nadu is under publication.

Ambai's writing exemplifies the voice of feminist self-affirmation in Tamil fiction. Her fiction presents experimentation in form (fables, prose-poems, monologues, surrealist pieces, expressionistic sequences—to mention a few), innovative, pluralistic narrative patterns, and an abundance of cultural allusions. Her writings suggest a continuous quest for freedom and self-fulfilment. They examine the complex ideological and gender trappings of a woman's identity and the need for female bonding. Ambai's writing abounds in images of freedom—of rivers, animals, the sea, fire, cooking, food, and flowers. She has evolved a language of her own, a new vocabulary, and a new style, constantly self-critical and ironic. A woman's consciousness of her sexuality, her history, and her place in society force Ambai to formulate a language of her own, in order to communicate not only with other women but also with a gender-biased society.

The dialectical journey between 'one's historical self and one's present society' which Ambai recommends for women writers is explored in 'Squirrel', originally published as 'Anil' in *Ini* (October 1986) and included in her second collection of stories, *Veetin Mulayil Oru Samayalarai* (A Kitchen in the Corner of the House, 1988). 'Squirrel' is a celebration of women and their writing. It is a writer's quest for the historicity of her self, and an elevation of the domestic to the literary, of detail to allusion. The narrator's enquiry into women's writing in the past takes her on a journey that blurs the distinction between dream and reality, past and present. 'Squirrel' is a piece of writing about writing—it thematizes a woman writer's literary history, her cultural auto/biography. The male librarian's dismissal of the tradition of women's self-empowerment through writing as 'mere trash' is juxtaposed with the narrator's almost erotic passion for those books. The motif of restoration, introduced through the reference to Ahalya, the food imagery indicating different kinds of appetite, the ambience of a sexual encounter at the beginning, and the fire imagery at the end are some of the clues for the exploration of this text which seeks to forge a bond between language, gender and identity. The story gains its resonance from a play between the dual possibilities of reading that it allows, involving a literal and a metaphorical probing of one's cultural heritage.

The translation reproduced here is by Lakshmi Holmström. Another translation, by Vasantha Kannabiran and Chudamani Raghavan *(Women Writing in India,* vol. 2, ed. Susie Tharu and K. Lalita, New Delhi: Oxford University Press, 1995), though closer to Ambai's prose rhythms, misses the humorous, teasing vocabulary of the conversations in the original. The narrator in the story uses a Brahminical urban variety of Tamil, while the librarian and his staff use Tamil that is identifiably non-Brahmin. These subtle variations are lost in English translation. Despite a few unwarranted elucidatory intrusions, Holmström's translation remains faithful to the original text.

SQUIRREL

Long verandahs of spacious buildings which were once the offices of the British government. The verandahs are enclosed by meshed windows with angled tops. At every ten feet, there are ornamental arches above. As one walks along, passing under the arches of that shadowy verandah where the sun does not enter, one experiences a sense of anticipation, that at the end of the darkness, there will be a library. Impossible to say why exactly, but one feels that expectation the moment one sets foot within the verandah. A quickening of the breath. A watering of the mouth. And often enough, it is there at the end, a library in truth. Yellowed. Stretched out in iron shelves.

One occasion. It was the time of year when it darkens early. The sun had only just set. As soon as I set foot in the verandah, there was a face as if suspended in space, floating in front of me. It was as if, starting from a pair of owl-like eyes, the flesh of the cheeks and neck had all slithered down like a waterfall. I was startled. I went cold. Then a few teeth appeared in a smile which pushed aside the wrinkled folds of skin.

'Were you frightened, madam?'

The light was switched on. A long verandah took shape. Endless archways. A sensation as if I was entering a cave. At the end of it, a soft red light shone behind a steel door, chequered all over with steel wires. Above and below the door, a reddish smoke spread. It seemed like a shadowy door leading to a different world. I imagined that the instant the door opened, I would see Urvashi dancing to the sound of her own anklet bells.

(Whatever narrow passage I entered, to me it became a verandah. I began to think that at the end of every path, there were only old books, lying on their backs, their tongues hanging out. If you picked one up, you'd find a dog-eared fold on the cover. Next to that a scratch. Heavy. Painful. Sometimes the spine of the book was broken by its own weight. If you touched it there, you heard a sudden snap. Each book that was stroked and awakened to life was a very Ahalya. But which epic was there that recorded its history?)

The phantom door stood in front of me as material reality. He opened it. There was a small garden path. At the end of that a heavy wooden door stood open.

'They've all gone. I waited for you to come. Here is the book you asked for.'

There was a sudden gust of wind. The pages rustled, beating against each other. When I put my hand on the cover, pressing it down, the trembling of the leaves passed into me. The old man was no longer beside me. Except for the light in the front part of the building, all the others had been turned off. Open iron shelving reached up to the high ceilings. Inside, there were two upper levels, with iron-sheeted floors, reached by an iron staircase. I was alone, my hand resting on the book. In the corner, by the door, the rustling of the pages set off by the wind now joined into a thud-thudding sound. It was then that it appeared before me. It sat upon a pile of books which had just been mended with paste. It threw me a brief glance and began to lick the paste with great enjoyment.

'Don't do that,' I said. 'That's *chintamani,* the women's journal that Balammal ran. That faded picture at the back, that's she in a nine-yard sari.'

(My relationship with her has only just begun. We have not yet conversed with each other. I don't as yet know everything about her, only that she was not all that fond of Vai Mu Ko.)

The squirrel listened. It took a quick look at Balammal and went away. The wind, the rustling of the pages and the throbbing under my fingers continued.

All this had happened so often, both in dream and in reality, that I could no longer separate one from the other. Neither did it seem all that important to do so. It was a fact that the pages crumbled and fell to pieces beneath my fingers. A fact that the crumbling bits stuck to my fingers. A fact that the apsaras who first advertised Kesavardini hair oil crumbled away with those pieces. But this happened many times, both in dreams and reality. That's why I didn't try to separate the two. When I was sure I was

dreaming, the electric fan would suddenly stop and I would find myself bathed in sweat. Certain that it was real, I would raise a book in order to smell it, and be awakened by the raindrops splashing on to my face through the open window. I didn't worry about it. Isn't it possible that some relationships should extend from dreams into reality, and others be the spillover from reality to dream?

A heavy dictionary, yellowing with age, lay upon a sloping desk by the window. When the wind blew, its huge pages would move. If I bent down, the pages touched my face. Moving, as if to stroke me, the pages would roll from 'B' to 'J'. And then the wind would stop. I would put it back to 'B'. One page alone would reach up to touch me affectionately on the cheek and then return to its place, leaving behind a faint smell.

I always move from one end of the open shelves to the other touching the books. Establishing a relationship. I touch the dust as if I were caressing a naked child. I share a relationship with all of you, did you know? It was my fingers that smoothed the crease running through the centre of the letter which Mary Carpenter wrote in the nineteenth century, asking to set up a women's teacher training college. It was I who blew off the rust-coloured dust which had spread over the 'Rani Victoria Kummi' published in *Viveka Chintamani.* When a speck of that dust flew up against my lip, I flicked out my tongue and swallowed it. And so an older generation descended into my stomach. Perhaps if some Yasoda had looked into my mouth, she would have seen a Victoria kummi.

It seemed that as soon as this library was set up, Krishna appeared in his chariot and preached his sermon of non-attachment there, giving as example the way water rolls off the lotus leaf. Nothing that the library contained touched anyone who was working here. Their only interest was in each one's knee-high stainless-steel tiffin carrier. On the third floor, the Buckingham Carnatic Mill workers went on strike in May 1921. But downstairs the concerns were different.

'Ei, have you brought meat today? It smells good.'

'Yes, di. I cooked minced meat this morning. We don't eat meat for the whole of the month of Purattaasi, and I have been feeling quite weak. My husband himself ground all the spices for me. But it's not yet time to eat. It's only twelve yet. Let's sit under the trees today. We'll take the water pot with us.'

'We could buy some betel leaf.'

'Watch out. Sir is coming.'

'Well, girls? Chatting about food are you? My wife says I must only eat fruit. She says I've got a paunch. I should have been lucky enough to be born a woman, to bear a couple of children and then to bloat out and wear a chokingly tight choli.'

'Sir, it's true you've actually got a bit of a paunch. Maybe that's why she says that.'

'I shall have to be born a woman in my next birth. Then my flesh can hang around my waist, like Elizabeth's.'

'Why this, Sir? Why do you drag me into all this? There is no malice in me, sir. That's why I'm not as thin as a stick.'

'Are you going out to buy betel leaf? Get me half a dozen fruit.'

'Jackfruit, do you mean, sir?'

'Who said that? People come to work in this place half dead with hunger. Doesn't like my paunch, she says. Why can't she show me even a spoonful of ghee? What's lost if some onion tossed in butter is spread on a bit of bread for me? Don't I toil hard enough through the day? Now, you lot...'

'What have we done, sir?'

'Get on with your work, girls. Five lakhs of books are waiting to be catalogued. That's enough about minced meat and husbands who grind spices.'

Laughter.

Kk...kwik.

It came and sat upon the Factory Act. Once again it screeched.

'Look here, you are an eater of nuts. What business do you have here? Aren't there enough trees outside? What's there for you in this paste? Go and climb a tree. Go up. Come down. What sort of bad habit is this?'

All of a sudden it spread out its four legs on the book and lay prone on its stomach. A ray of sunlight, refracted through a hole in the window mesh, struck it softly on the head. It closed its eyes.

I did not touch it. I have no faith in miracles. Even if I did, I would not put it to the test. I am not used to conversing with fairy princes.

The third floor was a somewhat neglected place. The man who catalogued Telugu books in one corner was given to muttering to himself every now and then. All the rest of the books were either torn, or just about to come apart, or had been pasted together in an effort to postpone death, and were waiting to be catalogued. The floor was of iron sheeting with a pattern of holes. Through these, you could see through to the ground floor. On one occasion, the book of chants used several years ago at the Madurai Meenakshi temple to exorcise evil spirits had slipped from my hands and fallen all the way down and on to the librarian's head.

And he had once climbed the ceiling-high open iron shelves in order to fulfil my wish, even forgetting his paunch.

'I can't reach to the top, sir, please look and tell me what there is up there.'

When he reached up there, he struck at the topmost stack of books with his hand. The dust rose in waves. When I craned my neck to look at him as he stood there, his legs spread apart and planted firmly on the shelves facing each other, his head immersed in clouds of dust, one hand pressed against his chest to prevent an imminent sneeze, he seemed like the good, obedient genie who appears and demands work at the merest rub of the magical lamp.

'What's up there, sir?'

'Dust... dust...'

'No sir, what books?'

'I'll look, madam. There are lots of good books written, though, without my having to climb up like this for them. This is all rubbish, madam, rubbish.'

'If you want, I'll climb up, sir.'

'No, no, madam. This is my duty.' He sneezed about ten times. 'These are all just women's books, madam. Do you want them?' 'Throw them down, sir.'

They fell with a thud. First, *Penmadhi Bodhini,* then *Jagan Mohini.* Several others followed. The notion of falling became closely linked in my mind with these books. It became an everyday occurrence to me to imagine them tearing their way through the roof and splitting their sides. For one who did not believe in miracles, I continued to experience a number of such illusions. When I touched the spine of an old mended nineteenth century book, an ecstatic tremor rose from the soles of my feet and passed through me, like an orgasm. When Anna Sattianadhan lay upon her deathbed, asking her husband to pray for her, there were only I and the squirrel on the third floor to share her grief. The

evangelist who rode horseback to propagate Christianity broke through the meshed windows of this same third floor. When a Bengali girl set fire to herself after leaving a note for her father, telling him he must not sell his only house in order to meet her marriage expenses, the flames chased through this very place, like snakes. The flames spread throughout the third floor and disappeared, having revealed their form only to the squirrel and me. The Telugu cataloguer was not there that day.

What the third floor contained was not just books, but a whole generation, throbbing with life. Respectable older women in nine-yard saris, with shoes upon their feet and rackets in hand, played badminton with white women. Many preached untiringly to younger women, how best they could please their husbands. They took great pains to explain the dharma that women should follow, addressing their readers as 'my girl', and putting on compassionate faces. Nallathangal chased her son even when he pleaded with her to let him go; pushed him into a well and jumped in after him. When a Brahmin stubbornly refused to do the last rites upon a girl who was an unshaven widow, her knee-length hair was removed from her very corpse. Devadasis dedicated to temples sang, 'I cannot bear the arrows of Kama,' as they danced to the point of exhaustion. Gandhi addressed women spinning at their charkas. Uma Rani of *Tyagabhumi* rang out, 'I am no slave.' In the women's pages, 'Kasini' wrote about new styles in bangles. The cover-girl of *Ananda Vikatan* swept along, swinging her arms while her husband carried her shopping bag. Taamaraikanni Ammal proclaimed, 'We will sacrifice our lives for Tamil.' Her real name— a Sanskrit one—was Jalajakshi. Ramamrutham Ammal confronted Rajaji head on when he wrote that Gandhi would not come unless he was paid money.

All, all these women were present there. And so was I. Sometimes they were weightless, as if made of smoke; at other times full of mass, heavy. The day the widow's head was shaven, a heaviness pressed upon my heart. Razor-blades appeared everywhere. Each lock of hair fell away with a loud sound. Each lock of hair rubbed abrasively against my cheek. I came to life only when the squirrel tapped its tail twice and raised the dust. It was leaning against the issue of *Kalki* which had Ammu Swaminathan on the cover. Apparently it had finished eating up the paste.

I looked downward through the holes in the floor. The librarian's head was eased back against the chair. On the desk, a file inscribed, Subject: STRING. This was his favourite file. Three years ago it had been a shining violet in colour: now it was fading and dog-eared. The file began with a letter requesting some string so that the old magazines could be sorted out and tied according to their months and years. Back came the answer that it was not customary to supply string to libraries and demanding a full explanation for breaking this rule. Following upon this were other letters. If the magazines were not separated according to their months, they became chaotic and useless. Useless to whom? To researchers. Which researchers? Were they from Tamilnadu or elsewhere? And so it went on. One day the librarian pulled out a ball of string from his trouser pocket. After this he wrote a letter asking to be reimbursed for the cost of a ball of string, which set off another series of letters. Every day the file would appear on his table. The money had still not been paid.

The squirrel screeched. Keech keech. My only link with reality. At the same time my companion in the world of illusions.

Yes, I know. It is late. The paste is finished. But I haven't the mind to leave these women. There seems to be a magical string that links us. I hear them speak. As Shanmuga Vadivu strikes the first note of the octave upon her vina, the sound floods into my ears. K. B. Sundarambal sings, 'Seeking the bright lotus, seeing it, the bee sings its sweet song... utterly lost.' And Vasavambal, accompanying her on the harmonium joins in, with 'utterly lost'. On the Marina beach, Vai Mu Ko hoists the flag of Independence. The women who oppose the imposition of Hindi go to prison, their babes in their arms.

Look, this is another world. That paste should have made you aware of at least a taste of it. A world which we share, you and I.

'Are you coming down, madam?' He was smiling as he looked up and called out.

'In a minute.'

He came up.

'We've been sent the Rule.' 'What Rule?'

'It's very expensive to mend and repair all this. Not many people read them either. Perhaps one or two like you. How can

the government afford to spend money on the staff and paste and so on? They are going to burn the lot.' 'Burn what?'

'Why, all these old unwanted books.'

Not a single thought rose in me. Except for one, at the edges of my mind. So the file on string has finally been closed. Only its burial is left now.

'Come, madam.'

I came to the iron stairs and then turned to look. The evening sun and the mercury lamp combined to spread an extraordinary light on the yellowing books, like the first flood of fire that spreads over a funeral pyre. Then he put out the light.

Darkness mingled with the dim red light, turning it into deep crimson, like magical flames. The squirrel lay prostrate in front of the window, its four legs spread out, in an attitude of surrender.

As I climbed down the stairs, a small wave of thought hit me: that window faces north.

Translated from the Tamil
by Lakshmi Holmstrom

ANNOTATIONS

Page 131
Urvashl: A heavenly nymph in Hindu mythology, renowned for her beauty and her skill in dancing.

Marks of parentheses on this page and on p. 132 are not there in the original text.

Page 132
Ahalya: Wife of the Rishi Gautama. She was seduced by Indra who deceived her into believing that he was her husband. The Rishi cursed her, turning her into a stone. In Pudumai Pittan's (1906–48) retelling of the legend in his story, 'Saba Vimochanam', Ahalya, on learning that Rama required Sita to undergo a trial by fire, chooses to turn into a stone again, rather than live in Ayodhya. *Chintamani:* A journal founded in 1924 by Sister Balammal for improving the condition of women and for disseminating knowledge among

them. A representative issue included articles on heroic Indian women, stories from the epics, and pieces of popular interest such as Marco Polo's travels.
Vai Mu Ko: Vai. Mu. Kodainayaki Ammal (1901–60): A Gandhian and one of the first Tamil women to wear and to advocate the use of khadi. She was also the editor of a journal, and a popular novelist who published more than 115 novels. She was married at the age of five and had no formal schooling. Her novels dealt with widow remarriage, the upliftment of Devadasis, and other social issues.

Page 133
Mary Carpenter: (1807–77). British philanthropist and social reformer who supported the movement for higher education for women. She established a National Indian Association to inform English opinion on the needs of India.
Rani Victoria Kummi: Kummi is a group dance performed by women on auspicious occasions. The dancers move in a circular pattern, clapping their hands rhythmically and singing songs. 'Rani Victoria Kummi' was a Kummi in praise of Queen Victoria. *Viveka Chintamani:* A journal founded in 1892 and edited by C.V. Swaminatha Iyer.
giving as example... lotus leaf: Here, the translator has expanded a cryptic idiomatic expression in the original. Kannabiran and Raghavan's translation reads: 'be like water on a lotus leaf, detached.'
Buckingham Camatic Mill... strike: When a British officer entered the mill with a revolver, one of the workers snatched the gun and ran away. A case of an attempt to murder was registered against the worker, and the mill was subsequently closed. The workers went on a hunger strike and were fired upon, resulting in the death of a woman worker. The Factory Act, mentioned later in the text, was formulated after this strike.
'di': A term of address used among women, indicating familiarity. In the original, the character uses a more affectionate term of address, 'aaamampa'. The closest corresponding term could be 'haan baba' in Hindi. There is no English equivalent. *Purattaasi:* A month in the Tamil calendar (late September to mid-October), considered holy by Hindus. The Navaratri festival is celebrated in Purattaasi, and it is customary not to eat onions, garlic and non-vegetarian

food during this month. It is also a month when special pujas are offered to Lord Venkateswara/Balaji of Tirupati.

Page 134
fairy princes: A reference to Rama caressing the squirrel on its back to appreciate its efforts during the construction of a bridge from Rameswaram to Lanka to rescue Sita. The squirrel is said to have got the three distinctive lines on its back when Rama caressed it.

Page 135
Penmadhi Bodhini: (Instructing Women's Minds). Founded in 1891, this was the first women's journal run by a woman, with articles written by women. The journal aimed at bringing reform, culture, and peace to women along with a knowledge of what they ought to do, so that they could lead happy married lives. *Jagan Mohini:* This journal was founded in 1924, and was edited by Vai. Mu. Kodainayaki Ammal. It had a large circulation of over 10,000 copies, and was even sold abroad.
Anna Satthianadhan: A converted Christian who set up a school to spread literacy among women. She was the mother-in-law of the novelist Krupabai Satthianadhan who wrote two novels which were serialized in a journal of the Madras Christian College.

Page 136
Bengali girl: An allusion to Snehalata, who committed suicide in the first decade of this century in Calcutta, protesting against dowry. Her marriage had been fixed by her parents after they had mortgaged their house to raise money for the dowry. Following Snehalata's death, many young men of Bengal took a pledge not to accept dowry.
Respectable older women... white women: 'Mamigal' (aunties) in the original. Upper class lawyers settled in Mylapore, Chennai, encouraged their wives and daughters to attend exclusive clubs where women wearing nine-yard sarees, shoes and socks would play badminton and other games. This was resented by many male writers who felt that these English games led to 'dangerous emotions', and that Tamil women would do well to restrict themselves to Kummi or to pounding rice for physical exercise. *Many preached... please their husbands:* Women's journals untiringly counselled women on

'good behaviour' and on 'karpu' (chastity), stressing docility and patience, and advising them that home indeed was the rightful place for women, and husbands the fit objects of worship.

Nallathangal: The protagonist of a popular Tamil tale which has been regularly and successfully dramatized over the years. She was the mother of six daughters and one son. Unable to bear the cruelty of her in-laws, she returned to her parental home. Her brother and sister-in-law taunted her by saying that it would be more honourable for her to jump into a well than to return to her father's house. Nallathangal pushed her daughters and her protesting son into a well. She cursed her father's clan that no daughter would ever be born into it to suffer like her, and ended her life. Her name, ironically, means 'good younger sister'.

When a Brahmin... corpse: Sister Subbalakshmi, a well-known social worker, was a widow who ran a home for Brahmin widows and provided education for them. To continue her work in the midst of orthodox protest, she had to concede to the demands made by the priestly class. The incident referred to here took place in her institution.

Devadasis: Young girls, especially those belonging to the Isai Vellala community, were married off to temple deities and were dedicated to serving in temples as classical singers and dancers, with many of them ending up as concubines of rich patrons of dance and music.

Kama: The God of love in Hindu mythology, similar to Cupid in Roman myths.

Tyagabhumi: Kalki's novel, serialized in the popular journal *Ananda Vikatan* in the 1930s, was made into a successful film. Uma Rani, the heroine, is a neglected wife who decides to get even with her husband in later years. She becomes rich and self-sufficient, and declares that she will not sacrifice her principles in exchange for slavery. The novel is set against the backdrop of the freedom movement, and the conclusion hints at a compromise between the estranged couple.

'Kasini': The pseudonym of a columnist who wrote about recipes and jewellery designs in the women's section of a journal. *Ananda Vikatan:* Founded in the 1930s, *Ananda Vikatan* (Happy Jester) has been a popular weekly till now. Its cover often carried jokes centred on women, with figures such as a dominating wife and a western-

ized shrewish wife. The cover of the issue of 19 September 1943 depicted a husband carrying countless parcels while his wife walks beside him swinging her arms.
Tamaraikanni Ammal: A prominent figure in the movement which emphasized the importance of Tamil and of Tamil culture, she translated her name, Jalajakshi, which in Sanskrit means 'lotus-eyed', into Tamil ('tamarai': lotus; 'kann': eye). In one of her stories, the heroine leads a group of picketeers to the school where her husband teaches Hindi and she then goes to jail. Love for Tamil, it is argued, has primacy over domestic duty. *Ramamrutham Ammal:* Belonged to the Devadasi community and played an active role, along with Dr Muthulakshmi Reddy, the first woman legislator, in abolishing the Devadasi system. Her novel, *Dasigalin Mosavalai Alladu Mathi Petra Minor* (The Seductive Net of the Devadasi or The Reformed Rake), published in 1936, is a stringent, rationalist argument against this system. *Kalki: A* journal run by R. Krishnamurthy, whose pen name was Kalki. It has remained popular to date. Ammu Swaminathan, a regular contributor to *Kalki,* was a freedom fighter and a Gandhian. She wrote on Gandhian thought.

Page 137
Shanmuga Vadivu: The daughter of the legendary musician, Veenai Dhanammal. The renowned classical singer M. S. Subbulakshmi is her daughter.
K. B. Sundarambal: A singer and an actress. She is remembered for her devotional songs and for her lead performances in the films, *Ouvvaiyar* and *Thiruvilayadal* (The Divine Leela of Muruga). *Vasavambal* accompanied her on the harmonium. *their babes in their arms:* The mass movement in Tamil Nadu against the imposition of Hindi as the national language was at its most militant in the early 1960s. Women's participation in this movement was more pronounced than in the earlier national struggle for independence.
madam: Inadequately translated throughout as 'madam', the Tamil word 'amma' is a form of address that signifies affection and respect. The word is used by men to address women, irrespective of age or class.

Page 138
The evening sun... funeral pyre: Fire imagery recurs in many of Am-

bai's stories. Her earlier story, 'Amma Oru Kolai Seydal' (Mother Commits a Murder), shows the merging of kitchen fire and sacrificial fire to indicate the protagonist's traumatic awareness of her entry into womanhood.

window faces north: The reference is to 'vadakkirutal', described in ancient Tamil poetry. It is a ritual of fasting unto death, facing northwards, undertaken in protest or sorrow. The food imagery deployed throughout the story culminates in a reference to a life-denying fast.

SUGGESTED READING

Holmstrom, Lakshmi, 'Introduction', *A Purple Sea,* New Delhi: AEWP, 1992.

Krishnankutty, Gita, *Ambai* (Katha Perspective), New Delhi: Katha, 1999.

Lakshmi, C. S., *The Face Behind The Mask: Women in Tamil Literature,* New Delhi: Vikas, 1984.

———, 'Tradition and Modernity of Tamil Women Writers', *Social Scientist* (April 1976), pp. 1–38.

Samanvitha, *Pioneer Women Writers of South India,* Bangalore: Department of Women's Studies, NMKRV College for Women, 1993.

Tharu, Susie and K. Lalita eds, *Women Writing in India* vol. 2, New Delhi: Oxford University Press, 1995.

FURTHER READING

GENERAL

Das, Sisir Kumar, *A History of Indian Literature, 1800–1910: Western Impact: Indian Response,* New Delhi: Sahitya Akademi, 1991.

———, *A History of Indian Literature, 1911–56: Struggle for Freedom: Triumph and Tragedy,* New Delhi: Sahitya Akademi, 1995.

George, K. M. ed., *Masterpieces of Indian Literature,* 3 vols, New Delhi: National Book Trust, 1997.

Kripalani, Krishna, *Modem Indian Literature: A Panoramic Glimpse,* Bombay: Nirmala Sadanand Publishers, 1968.

Mukherjee, Sujit ed., *The Idea of an Indian Literature: A Book of Readings,* Mysore: Central Institute of Indian Languages, 1981.

———, *Translation as Discovery and other Essays on Indian Literature in English Translation* (1981), new edn., Hyderabad: Orient Longman, 1994.

Paniker, Ayyappa, *Indian Literature in English,* Madras: Anu Chithra Publications, 1989.

JIBANANANDA DAS

Bandyopadhyay, Debiprasad ed., *Jibanananda Das: Bikash-Pratisthar Itibritta* [Jibanananda Das: A Critical Heritage], Calcutta: Bharat Book Agency, 1986 [A history of his reception among Bengali readers].

Bandyopadhyay, Saroj, *Kabitar Kalantar* [The New Age of Poetry], Calcutta: Sanyal Prakashan, 1976–7 [A study of Bengali poetry from the 1930s to the 1960s.]

Bose, Buddhadeva, *KalerPutul* [The Guardians of Time], Calcutta: New Age, 1959 [Essays on Bengali poets of the 1930s and the early 1940s].

Sengupta, Samarendra and Bhumendra Guha eds., *Bivav* (Jibanananda Special Centenary Issue), 20 (1999).

SRI SRI

Prasad, Chalasani, *Sri Sri Anantham* [Sri Sri Unending], Visakhapatnam:

Virasam, 1986 [A collection of Sri Sri's autobiographical essays and his reflections on literature].

Reddy, C. Narayana, *Adhunikandhra Kavitvamu: Sampradayamulu, Prayogamulu* [Modern Telugu Poetry: Tradition and Experiment], Vijayawada: Visalandhra Publications, 1969.

Rao, Velcheru Narayana, *Telugulo Kavita Viplavala Swarupam* [Forms of Revolution in Telugu Poetry], Hyderabad: Hyderabad Book Trust, 1987.

G. M. MUKTIBODH

Chauhan, Chanchal, *Muktibodh Ke Pratik Aur Bimb* [Muktibodh's Symbols and Images], New Delhi: Vani Prakashan, 1998.

Muktibodh, Gajanan Madhav, *Chand Ka Munh Terha Hai* [The Face of the Moon is Crooked], with an introduction by Shamsher Bahadur Singh, New Delhi: Bharatiya Jnanpith, 1964.

———, *Muktibodh Rachnavali,* 6 vols, ed. Nemichand Jain, New Delhi: Rajkamal Prakashan, 1980 [The Collected Works of Muktibodh].

Naval, Nandkishore, *Muktibodh: Gyan Aur Samvedana* [Muktibodh: Knowledge and Sensibility], New Delhi: Rajkamal Prakashan, 1993.

Sharma, Vishnu Chandra, *Muktibodh Ki Atamkatha* [Muktibodh's Autobiography], New Delhi: Radhakrishnan, 1994.

Singh, Bhagwan, 'Muktibodh Ki Kavitaon Ko Samajhane Ki Disha Mein Ek Prayatan' [An Attempt to Understand Muktibodh's Poems], in *Indradhanush Ke Rang* [The Colours of the Rainbow], New Delhi: Vani Prakashan, 1996, pp. 9–31.

Singh, Namwar, *Kavita Ke Naye Pratiman* [New Standards of Poetry]; New Delhi: Rajkamal Prakashan, 1974 (rpt. 1982).

NISSIM EZEKIEL

King, Bruce, *Modem Indian Poetry in English,* New Delhi: Oxford University Press, 1987.

Parthasarthy, R., 'Foregrounding as an Interpretative Device in Ezekiel's "Night of the Scorpion"', *The Literary Criterion,* 10, no. 3 (Winter 1974), pp. 38–44.

Patel, Gieve, 'Introduction', *Nissim Ezekiel: Collected Poems 1952–88,* New Delhi: Oxford University Press, 1992.

Rehman, Anisur, *Form and Value in the Poetry of Nissim Ezekiel,* New Delhi: Abhinav Publications, 1981.

Wiseman, Christopher, 'The Development of Technique in the Poetry of Nissim Ezekiel', *Journal of South Asian Literature,* 11, nos 3–4 (Spring-Summer 1976), Nissim Ezekiel Issue.

JAYANTA MAHAPATRA

Devy, G. N., 'Rites and Signs: A Note on Jayanta Mahapatra's Poetic Sensibility', in Madhusudan Prasad ed., *Living Indian English Poets: An Anthology of Critical Essays,* New Delhi: Sterling Publishers, 1989.

Mahapatra, Jayanta, *Selected Poems,* New Delhi: Oxford University Press, 1987.

———, 'The Stranger Within: Coming to Terms through Poetry', *Dalhousie Review,* 63 (1983).

———, Autobiographical essay, in *Contemporary Authors,* Autobiography Series, 9 ed. Mark Zadrozny, Detroit, Michigan: Gale Research Company, 1989.

PREMCHAND

Bajpeyi, Nanda Dulare, *Premchand: Sahityik Vivechan* [Premchand: A Literary Discussion], Jalandhar: Hindi Bhavan, 1956.

Gurtu, Shachirani ed., *Premchand Aur Gorky* [Premchand and Gorky], New Delhi: Rajkamal Prakashan, 1955.

Madan, Inder Nath ed., *Premchand: Ek Adhyayan: Jiwan, Chintan Aur Kala* [Premchand, A Study: His Life, Thought and Art], Banaras: Saraswati Press, n. d.

Markandey and Misra, S.P., *Premchand Ki Kahaniyon Ka Mahatva* [The Importance of Premchand's Stories], Allahabad: Sumit Prakashan, 1998.

Sharma, Ram Vilas, *Premchand Aur Unka Yug* [Premchand and His Age], New Delhi: Rajkamal Prakashan, 1993.

R. K. NARAYAN

Dwivedi, A. N. ed., *Studies in the Contemporary Indian English Short Story,* New World Literature Series, 38, Delhi: B. R. Publishing Corporation, 1990.

Iyengar, K. R. Srinivasa, *Indian Writing in English,* 4th edn., New Delhi: Sterling Publishers, 1984.

Macaulay, Thomas B., 'Minute on Indian Education' (1835), in *Speeches of Lord Macaulay with His Minute on Indian Education,* selected with an introduction and notes by G. M. Young, Oxford: Oxford University Press, 1935.

Mukherjee, Meenakshi, *The Twice-Born Fiction,* New Delhi: Heinemann, 1971.

Naik, M. K., *A History of Indian English Literature,* New Delhi: Sahitya Akademi, 1982.

Rao, Raja, 'Foreword', *Kanthapura,* New Delhi: Oxford University Press, 1989.

Venugopal, C. V., *The Indian Short Story in English: A Survey,* Bareilly: Prakash Book Depot, 1976.

VAIKOM MUHAMMAD BASHEER

Ashraf, E. M, *Vaikom Muhammad Basheer,* Kottayam: D.C. Books, 1994 [A biography].

——— ed., *Basheerinte Airavathangal* [Basheer's Sacred Elephants], Trissur: Current Books, 1990 [A selection of critical writings on Basheer].

Achutan, M., *Cherukatha: Innale, Innu* [The Short Story: Yesterday and Today], Kottayam: S. P. C. S., 1973 [A history of the short story in Malayalam].

Basheer, Vaikom Muhammad, *Basheer: Sampoorna Krithikal* [Basheer: Complete Works], 2 vols, 2nd edn., Kottayam: D. C. Books, 1999.

Vijayan, M. N. *Marubhoomikal Pookkumbol* [When Deserts Bloom], Kasarkode: Kalakshetram, 1994.

SAADAT HASAN MANTO

Alvi, Waris, *Saadat Hasan Manto,* New Delhi: Sahitya Akademi, 1995 [A monograph on Mantp in Urdu].

Hasan, Mushirul, *India Partitioned: The Other Face of Freedom,* 2 vols, New Delhi: Roli Books, 1985.

Mahajan, Sucheta, 'Freedom and Partition', Bipin Chandra et al., *India's Struggle for Independence,* New Delhi: Viking/Penguin, 1987.

Manto, Saadat Hasan, *Dastavez* [A Literary Document], ed. Balraj Manra and Sharad Datt, 5 vols, New Delhi: Rajkamal Prakashan, 1993 [A collection of Manto's stories, letters and essays in the Devanagari script].

ISMAT CHUGHTAI

Chughtai, Ismat, *Kaaghazi Hat Pairahan* [The Apparel is Paper-Thin], Delhi: Rajkamal Prakashan, 1998 [Chughtai's Autobiography].

Wadhawan, Jagdish Chandra, *Ismat Chughtai: Shaksiyat Aur Fan* [Ismat Chughtai: Her Personality and Art], Delhi: Jagdish Chandra Wadhawan, 1996.

AMBAI

Geetha, 'Samayalari Mulayil Oor Ulakam' [A World in a Kitchen-Corner],

Kalachchuvadu, 2 (April-June 1989), pp. 43–5.

Vannanilavan and others, 'Chirakukal Mulaikkum: Ambaiyudan Oru Sandippu' [Wings Do Grow: An Encounter with Ambai], Part 1, *Kalachchuvadu,* 19 (October–December 1997), pp. 23–34.

———, 'Ellaigal, Meeralgal: Sandippu—Ambai' [Boundaries, Transgressions: Encounter—Ambai], Part 2, *Kalachchuvadu,* 20 (January–March 1998), pp. 25–40.